# REFORMING THE SCHOOLS

## for Teachers

John W. Friesen
The University of Calgary

UNIVERSITY
PRESS OF
AMERICA

Lanham • New York • London

British Cataloging in Publication Information Available

**Library of Congress Cataloging-in-Publication Data**

Friesen, John W.
    Reforming the schools—for teachers.

    Includes bibliographies.
    1. School improvement programs—United States.
2. School improvement programs—Canada.    3. Teachers—
United States.    4. Teachers—Canada.    I. Title.
II. Title: Reforming the schools.
LB2822.82.F75    1987        371.2'07        87-13361
ISBN 0-8191-6479-8 (alk. paper)
ISBN 0-8191-6480-1 (pbk. : alk. paper)

to my daughter,
 Gaylene Joan Martens,
 one of my favorite teachers

# ACKNOWLEDGEMENTS

As with any work of this magnitude, there are a number of individuals who have labored behind the scenes in bringing this book to completion. Although it is impossible to name all of them, I would be remiss if the following persons were not mentioned: Miriam Zachariah, who did much of the library research; Edith Elizabeth Wieler, who edited most of the text; Jeanne Keech who typed the various editions of the manuscript, and Karen Gagaluk who made the final corrections. I must also acknowledge a grant from Alberta Manpower which aided in completing the research, and thank the students in my first-year course, "Introduction to Teaching," whose interest provided motivation and inspiration.

Finally, I am grateful to the Department of Education Policy and Administrative Studies at The University of Calgary for furnishing an environment in which my research interests can be pursued. In the final analysis, however, the content of this book is mine and I am prepared to answer for it.

John W. Friesen
The University of Calgary
May, 1987

# REFORMING THE SCHOOLS -- FOR TEACHERS

## Table of Contents

CHAPTER

      Introduction ................................. vii

One    THE PENDULUM OF EDUCATIONAL CHANGE    1

Two    REFORM AND CHANGE:
      FOR BETTER OR WORSE? ..................... 31

Three    PROFESSIONALS AND NON-PROFESSIONALS:
      WHO'S IN CHARGE HERE? .................... 50

Four    ALTERNATIVE SCHOOLING:
      SYMPTOM OF DISEASE OR CURE? ............ 67

Five    DELIVERING ON THE DOLLAR:
      EDUCATION AS A COMMODITY .............. 89

Six    SCHOOL REFORM FOR TEACHERS:
      CAN WE PLAY TOO? ........................ 116

Seven    TOWARDS AUTONOMY:
      THERE IS A BETTER WAY ................... 140

# REFORMING THE SCHOOLS - FOR TEACHERS

## Introduction

In February, 1986, Harper's Magazine sponsored a debate on educational reform, entitled, "How Not To Fix The Schools". The published result featured the opinions of Albert Shanker, Theodore Sizer, Ernest Boyer, Floretta McKenzie, Dennis Littky, Mark Danner, Ivan Krakowshy, A. Graham Down, and Walter Karp. Interestingly, most of the panelists are educators and include a principal, a superintendent, a high school teacher, and a professor of education. This lends a definite credibility to the group.

Central to the discussion was a report on America's schools called A Nation at Risk, which was prepared by the National Commission on Excellence in Education. Not surprisingly, the report lamented the "perilous condition of America's schools", quickly gained a following among state legislators and even became a topic of presidential debates. In the year that followed, forty-one states undertook measures to upgrade their educational standards by incepting more rigorous student evaluation and testing programs, requiring additional instruction time in schools, and, in general, increasing the workload of the teacher.

The reforms motivated by the report had two essential characteristics. First, they were originated and imposed by persons outside the educational operation (politicians, mainly), and they were structural or technical in nature. This action reflected American concerns to localize education but it also revealed a somewhat reactionary stance. Rather than concentrate on the weaknesses of an inadequate delivery system, if there indeed was one, the impulse was to "move the furniture around". Often, the realization, "Dear me, our kids can't read," is followed by a quick trip to the legislation to lengthen the school day.

Proposed educational reforms tend to reflect fairly standard approaches - money, accountability, student achievement, and, on rare occasion, educational philosophy. In the latter case the procedure is usually to develop alternative or private school systems or perhaps to ignore the institution altogether by opting for home schooling. Financial concerns frequently emanate from the "businessman's approach to learning", i.e. are children learning as fast as they can or as much as they can for every dollar spent? This line of attack fails to take cognizance of any developments in psychology or the social sciences which focus on such concepts as learning readiness, student individuality, health of the student or even aptitude. A certain number of students being detained in a classroom for a specified number of hours ought to produce a certain amount of achievement. Primary targets for related reforms subsequently deal with curriculum content, evaluation and measurement of results and length of the school day or the school year.

What has been learned about the process of teaching and learning in the last several decades casts doubt on the merits of the "business" approach because schooling involves people. They may be "little people" in most cases, but they still manifest the characteristics of humanity. They are complex creatures who function in and contribute to developments in the area of technology and in the area of human relations. Their perceptions and indeed accomplishments may be determined by time and place, mood or status of health.

A key factor in effective education is the role of the teacher. Here again, studies have shown that teachers are affected by their own psychological assessments and "readiness to teach" which status is further influenced by any number of factors. Primary among these is how teachers view their working environment, how they feel about their social and professional positions and, more importantly, how they feel about themselves. Effective teachers generally experience positive feedback from their reference groups, namely administration, students and parents, and convey their appreciation for positive assessments in their manner of delivery. Happy teachers are also effective teachers.

It has been said many times that teachers are the key to good education. If this is so, the insights gleaned from the literature on effective functioning should tell us that educational reform should be directed at teaching. What kinds of changes are required in the school systems as we know them that will improve or alleviate the lot of the teacher? Their work place and work load ought to be the primary target of educational reform.

This book provides a response to that challenge. As a means of illustrating how the teaching profession has been bypassed or overlooked in reform movements, several reform plans are examined in the initial chapters, and the root of their platforms revealed. Basically, these have aimed at rearranging the furniture of existing programs and directing attention toward pretty well every facet of education other than the teacher. If that profession is addressed at all in reform plans the end result is additional responsibilities for the profession.

The plan of autonomous education described in this book does two things. It introduces a reform package targetted at the teaching area of schooling with a view to amending the current situation so as to encourage the potential and to utilize the maximum capabilities of the profession. Second, it also poses a challenge to teachers by calling on them to mobilize their forces and energies toward producing quality education. This challenge has a number of legal and economic implications, but it is founded on the premise that the teaching profession can and will deliver quality education only when its constituents are awarded and when they claim the professional territory that is rightfully theirs. Thus, the key to quality education now is to reform schooling with the teacher in mind. We have tried everything else and possibly overlooked the most vital component to educational efficiency.

Better late than never!

Chapter One

# THE PENDULUM OF EDUCATIONAL CHANGE

> So I went down to the potter's house, and I saw
> him working at the wheel. But the pot he was
> shaping from the clay was marred in his hands; so
> the potter formed it into another pot, shaping it as
> seemed best to him.
>
> Jeremiah 18:3-4

The institution of schooling was hardly established when criticism of its operations became a popular pasttime. Throughout its rather brief history, various factions have tried to redirect the course of school instruction, usually by recommending a change in objectives, content or teaching approach. At times the initial call for change has been singular, like that of a lone voice crying in the wilderness, but frequently the forces have rallied to incorporate national concerns which have effected significant alterations in schooling.

It is not surprising that schools are a target for analysis or attack. First, it is because they involve the care and socialization of the young, who are thought of as a nation's most prized possession; second, they are viewed as a viable agency for social reform since they are primarily concerned with learning; and third, they are perceived as a ripe target for marketting a variety of innovative business products. In the context of reform, schools are targetted for social, economic or political interests because "everyone thinks" that the school is responsible for handling problematic phenomena. In fact, many schools do attempt to meet that challenge, although there is increasing evidence to suggest that there are other things for the school to undertake. Its mandate is essentially to prepare the young for adult life rather than to promote social reform. The case may be that if reform is to be undertaken, it should perhaps be intra-school rather than societal.

There are three historical perspectives from which educational reforms have usually originated, each of them surfacing just before the turn of the century. These are traditionalism, vocational, and progressivism. The three approaches have focussed on the rudiments of the learning process without paying any mind to the needs of the developing teaching profession. While outlining the major foci of these positions, it will be possible to demonstrate the central concerns for most school reform proposals and build a

1

case for the identification of emerging professional needs.

The traditional perspective on schooling has consistently defended the aims which were drafted when the institution was originated (the three "R's" etc.), and its main components included what could fundamentally be called socialization. The procedures by which this process was carried out were memorization and rote and the classics furnished the content. Mental discipline was a much revered notion with the addendum conceptualization that if the process of learning could be made difficult, it would somehow be more memorable and worthwhile. Some individuals who still remember the days when that process was in vogue can testify to its lingering cognitive value, even though the memory may be more negative than positive.

Mental discipline and faculty psychology both have their roots in the European tradition propounded by such thinkers as the English philosopher, John Locke. Locke suggested that the "gentleman" could be produced via rigorous processes that included the careful selection of sense data to impact on the child's "blank tablet mind". Sensations would produce ideas and then habits, which would guarantee the formation of proper character. Early North American educators promulgated this approach but two questioning bodies of thought surfaced at the end of the nineteen-hundreds. One of these was vocationalism, which was characterized by a concern about educational preparation for the business world, arguing that a mental wrestle with the classics produced a fixation for abstractions rather than furnishing marketable employable skills. Almost simultaneously, the progressivist forces led by John Dewey evolved the principle of educating "the whole child" by utilizing life experiences as a valuable adjunct to the curriculum. Dewey and his compatriots were resoundly accused of going soft on education, and encouraging children to indulge their fantasies and urges by providing no structure for their educational activities. Naturally, Dewey countered these claims, arguing that if children were allowed to express themselves entirely without guidance, any meaningful growth would be merely accidental.[1]

The juxtaposing of the three streams of thought continued in North American education for the decades before the nineteen sixties when a new series of onslaughts began highlighting the ideas of the radical humanists, the abolitionists and those promoting a social conscience for the school. The see-saw effect which the continual juxtaposing of three major philosophies inveyed on the schooling process was

2

further complicated by a variety of factors, not the least of which was persistent and charismatic leadership. A brief delineation of the three positions will serve to substantiate this thesis.

An analysis of the essence of schooling in early North America shows it to be an extension of the American home. The early pilgrims, the Loyalists, who later migrated to Canada, and the settlers who came west all began schools with a similar intent, namely to afford their children the benefits of basic literacy. The economic conditions of the times dictated that schools be simply constructed with an uncomplicated curriculum. The three R's took up most of the time with a healthy dose of religion thrown in. Later, schooling became national business and eventually attracted the attention of educators and politicians alike. Educators wondered aloud about the possibilities of schooling in terms of its applicability to life and politicians speculated about ways to utilize the schools as a means of fostering national loyalties. Once implemented, the change process became somewhat of a national rite.

## PROGRESSIVE EDUCATION

The first significant campaign against the mundane operations of the classic one-room schoolhouse came from the progressivists. Not content with the preoccupation of the school with teaching the rudiments of literacy and assuring the inculcation of prevailing norms, the progressivists were concerned with the individual child. They wanted children's needs to be met, their interests accounted for, and their feelings and attitudes considered in determining curriculum activities. This meant that the role of the teacher would be redrafted to that of a guide or facilitator rather than an imparter of truth, and the student would become an active participant in a problem-solving process rather than an absorber of content. The reformers were also concerned about classroom atmosphere, arguing that harsh punishment and rigidity were not as conducive to learning as an understanding and supportive orientation on the part of the teacher. Learning procedures would also have to be modified to allow for and to encourage student input based partially on life experiences and partly on "research" conducted by the student.

The underlying assumptions for these proposals startled the educational world to a new reality. John Dewey actually believed children had something to offer the educational process and he was prepared to take steps to incorporate their insights. In searching for appropriate furniture for his laboratory school at the University of Chicago in 1897, Dewey was informed that the only kind of desks available were those in which students could "listen rather than work". Rows of desks were bolted together and moved in rows. That, apparently, was what good education was all about.[2] The grounds on which Dewey made his defense of student input included entirely different concepts of human nature and learning than had previously been acknowledged. He conceptualized learning as an interactive process in which the learner moves on his environment, social or material, and is influenced by it in a reciprocal fashion. Learning, hence, is not a passive matter with children resembling milk bottles to be filled at some processing plant. He conceived of truth and value in the same sense, allowing for the interpretations of man to influence what "really is", if it can be known, claiming that individuals act not according to what is known but according to the way they perceive each confronting situation.[3] Dewey similarly redefined human nature in terms of a basic neutrality, suggesting that the traditional notion of depravity or moral deprivation were basically reflective of cultural interpretations.

A fundamental commitment to democracy was also central to progressivism. The concomitant objective was to promote an environment where even the "least" would feel welcome; the plan would be to build a society where "men with minor gifts of the intellect can feel equality in all their claims for development and a decent life, can escape exploitation, use their faculties with a feeling of self-respect, gain the reward they deserve, and live as citizens . . ."[4] An irritant to the progressivists was the exclusivity of nineteenth century education which featured the selection of students strictly by academic achievement. Their interpretation of democratic education was that a maximum of common experience and a minimum of segregation is desirable, and both academic and vocational education should be postponed until students were of the age where selection would be better justified.[5] Some progressivists were entirely against selection of any variety.

The child-centred approach promulgated by the progressivists found ample support in the advancement of the social sciences including child study and adolescent psychology. Correctly interpreted, it was not a campaign for children's rights, but rather belief in the ability of individuals of a very young age to become self-governing[6]; the point was that the process should be introduced gradually, not merely on attaining adulthood. Central to the concept was a healthy respect for the child, respecting and

4

accepting him as he is, first, because he is a human being, and second, because the child has already accomplished feats of growing, the like of which the teacher may never achieve, and third, because he has the potential to make a contribution to mankind.[7] The process by which to assure this development was through inquiry - differentiating, analysing, ordering, and synthesizing experience rather than merely listening, writing and regurgitating.[8]

In progressivist influenced schools, curriculum content switched quickly to a study of problems, issues and social trends as a means of acquainting the child with his immediate world. The grounds on which these phenomena evolved, namely values, were also given consideration even to the extent of questioning the nature of values, selection of fundamental values, the classification of values, value standards, and whether values are merely subjective desires or whether there is some law or norm applicable to desire.[9] Opposition to this approach arose quickly, critics claiming that students should be taught content rather than process, and, further, they could hardly be meaningfully engaged in solving social problems at such a young age. The traditional purpose of schooling was to prepare students for the world they would eventually participate in as adults; it was not a place to play grown up games.

If the critics were harsh with the progressivists, their campaign was at least partially motivated by the radical departures they made with established intellectual routines. On the more extreme edge of the movement were the reconstructionists who frightened the public even more with their announcements to build a new social order via schooling. This was certainly no way to exploit the traditional bastian of socialization and the critics minced neither words nor time in promoting that opinion.

Building a New Social Order

Few articles in the Progressive Education Association's journal, The Social Frontier, were as controversial as those authored by George S. Counts, Harold Rugg, William H. Kilpatrick, and John L. Childs, largely because they conceptualized education as responsible for the development of a society more responsive to individual needs. Although The Social Frontier never printed a statement that clearly delineated the specific goals of the social reconstructionists, Counts and his colleagues made it clear what their visions for the future were. Essentially, the group was directly concerned with the moral effect of capitalism on the person;

they believed that the profit motive had a particularly pernicious effect on individual morality. Kilpatrick was especially critical of this trend and wanted to create a new system of social values that would alter the manner in which society distributes its wealth.[10] Counts agreed that schooling cannot rest with giving children an opportunity merely to study contemporary society but also to lead them to becoming active in molding the future. This could best be accomplished through encouraging their contemplative and visionary capabilities. Truly the philosopher, Counts was not very precise in explicating his own ideals for the new social order, stressing only that students be given opportunity to participate in the fullest and most thorough understanding of the world. No suppression or distortion of facts supporting any theory or point of view should occur in their analysis of social problems. Counts castigated the view that mankind is the victim of rapid social change and helpless to do anything about it. He conceded that the forces of massive technicalizations have a way of appearing to outwit man by the very machines he has created, and ached for the development of an enlightened citizenry to take charge of both their present and future. Such an orientation could only be assured via the inauguration of the problem-solving process in early education as well as maintaining a dedication to the concept of life-long learning.[11]

About a decade after the social reconstructionists emerged, educator-philosopher Theodore Brameld reaffirmed their message by emphasizing a new urgency and an enlarged agenda to include such topics as international conflict, overpopulation, use of national resources, and other encompassing crises. He envisaged the eventual development of a world civilization and projected the quick formation of world government and a universal educational system to pave the way for what he saw as both logical and inevitable. The fundamental premises of this undertaking would include respect for human dignity, and respect for all races, castes, and classes. Brameld was prepared to explicate both objectives and curriculum for this monumental undertaking, never flinching in the face of criticism that he was proposing an unrealistic and possibly naive attitude toward the potential of education in resolving world issues.[12]

The Canadian Connection

Although the progressive education movement made much less extensive inroads on the Canadian educational scene, there were voices that paid tribute to many of the basic assumptions of the theory. In Alberta, Hubert Newland spoke to many audiences extolling the virtues of such concepts as education as growth, child development as total rather than segmental, and goal-centred education, offering Canadians much the same fare as Dewey and his associates were in the U.S.A. A classroom teacher, Donalda Dickie, designed a project-centred curriculum approach known as the enterprise method which reflected progressivist ideas but fell short of developing direct links to the underlying philosophy of education. In Nova Scotia, Loren De Wolfe placed great stress on what he called "experience-centred" education, even though his constituents were more concerned about the applications of learning to making a living in that region of the country. De Wolfe incorporated a real concern for teacher education and welfare in his portfolio of reform, even though his efforts fell short of any analysis of either the profession's status or authority. Insofar as the implementation of progressivist ideas in Canada was concerned, the situation could best be described as a fragrance that permeated the nostrils of the enterprise of schooling without seriously affecting its direction or makeup. There is ample evidence, however, that today's educational atmosphere in Canada is more receptive to progressivist ideas than it was when the movement was in vogue.[13]

## TRADITIONALISM IN EDUCATION

The initial opposition to progressivist education originated with the defenders of the old regime who feared any deviation from what they perceived to be "good education". Their defence led to a tightening of their grip on schooling and a retrenching of established practices. Some of the antagonists who called for a revival of the old ways included Arthur Bestor, James Koerner, Max Rafferty and Hilda Neatby.

In 1953 Arthur E. Bester wrote a book called Educational Wastelands[14] in which he decried the inroads made by the progressivists. Bester was particularly concerned that the intellectual elements of education be preserved, and he complimented America for spending so much money on schooling as assurance of the nation's sincerity about providing a high standard of education. He saw the threat of progressivism as watering down the essence of education whose prime purpose is to teach students how to think. This ability cannot be developed in a vacuum. It is possible only through the teaching of something to think about - of content. That content must be mastered, purely and simply. It cannot be substituted with "process", as the progressivists

7

contend.[15]

Equally vocal to Bester, Max Rafferty promoted the value of teaching the three "R's", and religion and patriotism, and bemoaned the progressivists' emphasis on educational frills and "life adjustment". Rafferty waged a war for content in curriculum, claiming that good english was as hard to come by in America as a sound educational philosophy. The contamination of history and geography as civics and economics had also thrown those fields into a slump of understanding that would render students illiterate for generations to come.[16]

In elaborating his own premises on education, Rafferty identified a number of myths which he preferred to see dispelled, e.g. the notion that schools exist to adjust pupils to their environment, that school curriculum should be based on the immediate interests and felt needs of the pupils, that memorizing things in school is hopelessly stultifying or that school policy should be set by school staff and students.[17] For Rafferty, the traditional way was best. "Stress subject matter", he pled, "all subject matter, provided it has been placed in the curriculum of the schools by the representatives of the people."[18]

James D. Koerner took his campaign against the life adjustment concept to the arena of teacher education. He argued that high standards of learning could be restored in the nation's schools only if more attention was given to demanding such in teacher training. He accused the American educational system of being almost entirely devoid of a philosophy of education in the sense of deriving methodological principles from carefully identified philosophical premises, and accused John Dewey of making only a few discernible bridges between his philosophy and his educational ideas. Koerner was not convinced that a lessening of academic rigour in the nation's classrooms as the progressivists urged would do anything to promote the development of a more comprehensive or systematic philosophy of education.[19] Koerner may have been correct on that point, but his accusations against Dewey were certainly off base. Dewey continually warned against the practice of adopting teaching methods on a whim, and consistently pled for teachers to examine the underlying premises of any so-called new approach.

There was no dearth of critics of progressivism on the Canadian scene, many of them focussing on teacher education. Frank MacKinnon peddled the popular myth that "anyone

8

could get into education" and compared education's entrants with the business world which, allegedly, education majors tried to avoid. He also made comments on the lack of scholarship in education faculties, the contamination of course content and the powerlessness of teacher associations and unions. MacKinnon's solution to the dilemma of poor quality in the educational delivery system was to upgrade teacher training so that its graduates would be capable of assuming greater responsibility in the classroom. MacKinnon's stance was not entirely without sympathy for the teaching role and he suggested that too much control and glory for success normally falls to the state and to school administration instead of to teachers. If he had been able to upgrade the quality of the profession he appeared to be quite willing to advance them more respectability and responsibility.[20] Hilda Neatby of the University of Saskatchewan was less generous, contending that very little good could come of the teaching profession since its spokespeople had done so much to denigrate quality education. A favored Neatby target was the "educational expert" whom she described as a symbol of the times in the sense of that position merely reflecting a general lowering of standards and a "going soft" in Canadian society. Although Neatby has a special disdain for educational jargon and humanization of the curriculum, she also envisaged a "revival of civilization" (parallel to that sketched by Theodore Brameld, one of her arch enemies) through the return of scholarship and academia in the schools.[21] Reformers, it appears, regardless of their philosophical ties, are quite shackled by the tendency to go in circles.

## The Great Books Approach

Critics and dissenters aside, the traditional education movement also attracted a group of serious-minded reformers who ably outlined the way to return to the basics as a means of salvaging society, i.e. the Great Books approach. Best known, perhaps, was Robert Hutchins of the University of Chicago, with Jacques Maritain and Mortimer Adler adding a concern for the spiritual component of the intellectual pursuit.

Adler's work furnishes a good starting point for the discussion, particularly his contribution to the 41st Yearbook of the National Society for the Study of Education wherein he described the ultimate ends of all education as being "the same for all men at all times and everywhere". Adler railed on the progressivist notion that experience is a valuable commodity in the learning process claiming that only a study of the "great ideas" would liberate the human mind. These

9

ideas are universal, transcultural and capable of motivating discussions of the highest order of reason. Adler maintained that absolute universal principles could be identified and proven - absolute in the sense that philosophy is not relative to the contingent circumstances of time and place, and universal in the sense that it is concerned with essentials and abstracts from every sort of merely accidental variation.[22] Thus the derivation of a philosophy of education is entirely dependent upon a knowledge of the first principles from which aims and methodologies spring. These singularly reside in the great ideas of human civilization.

Adler's classic work, How To Read A Book,[23] reflected the traditionalists' complaint that the progressivists failed to promote high academic standards. Under progressivism, tests of high school graduates revealed some of them unable to pass minimal tests of literacy. Although Adler had personally been a student of John Dewey, he found the ideas of his mentor, Robert M. Hutchins, more plausible and joined him in compiling the "Great Books" collection. He was also instrumental in developing the Syntopicon as an index to the main ideas of the Great Books.

Although the traditionalists who espoused the Great Books criticised the progressivists for the use of mushy language, their own vocabulary sometimes failed to connect with the expectations of the educational layman. Perhaps that was the intent because only the "Great Minds" would comprehend it anyway. Consider this morsel:

What is liberal education? . . . It is not an education that teaches a man how to do any specific thing. . . . This is what liberal education is. It is the education that prepares us to be free men. You have to have this education if you are going to be happy; for happiness consists in making the most of yourself. You have to have this education if you are going to be a member of the community; for membership in the community implies the ability to communicate with others. You have to have this education if you are going to be an effective citizen of a democracy; for citizenship requires that you understand the world in which you live and that you do not leave your duties to be performed by others, living vicariously and vacuously on their virtue and intelligence. A free society is a society composed of free men. To be free you have to be educated for freedom.[24]

Hutchins and his colleagues demonstrated an unshakable faith in the power of reason derived from knowledge as a basis for social reform. Hutchins also argued that if the school were to be charged with a particular program of reform, such an effort would represent nothing more than the sum total of the ideas of those who propounded it. Therefore, reform should be designed on a sound platform. He agreed with Plato that even "governments reflect human nature", which itself is predicated on universal knowledge and not subject to time and space (or place) and if pursued, must constitute the basis of man becoming what only he is capable of becoming, namely free.[25]

Hutchins took quite a ribbing for some of his ideas but he retaliated with unsustained vigor. Basically, he was accused of being a moral idealist - an absolutist in a time when relativity was on a high roll. Hutchins, like Dewey, propounded the principle that metaphysics must play an important role in the determination of educational aims because metaphysical beliefs comprise the drawing board from which content and approach are framed. By way of deduction from his premises, Hutchins concluded that the aim of education was wisdom and goodness and any studies that do not lead to that goal are fallacious.[26] Dewey would have agreed with the importance of deriving practical action programs from metaphysical assumptions, but his list differed significantly from Hutchins because the a priori assumptions from which the two thinkers started were poles apart. Moreover, the two were not sufficiently on speaking terms so that any differences could be examined or compared.

Of primary concern to American educators generally is the concept of democracy, and equally so with the traditionally-minded liberalists. Their position was in stark contrast to that of the progressivists. Dewey's passion for equal opportunity led him to support the notion of heterogeneous grouping in schools so that the less able would be able to benefit from their more knowledgeable peers. Adler, on the other hand, readily admitted that since individuals are not equally intelligent at birth, nor will they ever become so, all people are at least educable to the point of becoming good citizens.[27] This position would accommodate the principle of "government by the people" but did not impede the development of those with leadership potentialities beyond those of the average "educable citizen". Dewey must have cringed at that one!

11

## Still Another Viewpoint

For several decades the war among the major philosophical camps raged on with little hope for any reconciliation. A synthesis was finally proposed by Jerome S. Bruner in his little volume, The Process of Education[28] which emerged from the Woods Hole Conference in Massachusetts in 1959. Bruner argued that children could justifiably be confronted with the rudiments of a basic liberal education early in their development; in other words, any subject can be taught effectively in some intellectually honest form to any child at any stage of development. He agreed with the progressivists that a child should be assisted in the process of discovery learning, while maintaining that a good curriculum also stresses structure, but not details. Structure implies that all content is related which is different from the notion that curriculum is a series of discrete pieces of knowledge. Individuality in education is accommodated by encouraging students to discern relationships between elements of knowledge personally. Once the structural concept is comprehended, the student will be able to transfer his understanding to other areas of interest. Always his objective will be to seek structure (relationships) within all fields of his experience. Equipped with structural insight, the student will be able to efficiently and effectively utilize whatever specific information is at hand.[29]

Traces of Deweyianism are evident throughout Bruner's treatise, particularly when he suggests principles like, "intellectual growth involves an increasing capacity to say to oneself and others, by means of words or symbols, what one has done or what one will do," and "growth depends upon internalizing events into a 'storage system' that corresponds to the environment."[30] Clearly, the earmarks of respect for individualized insight is evident in Bruner's principles, but his underlying conceptualization of a "basic" structure of incorporated knowledge (which is metaphysically "outside of the student") should go a long way toward appeasing the traditionalist's notion of absolute knowledge.

## Adding A Religious Component

Although the traditionalists made a great deal of the notion of absolute truth and knowledge, only a few writers made allowances for the emanation of truth from Theistic sources. Hence it was left to the Neo-Thomists, revivalist followers of Thomas Acquinas, to add that component to the discussion. Best known was the abbreviated work of Jacques Maritain who delivered the memorable Terry Lectures at Yale

University in the early forties which were published in a small book, Education At The Crossroads.[31] Essentially anti-progressivist, Maritain lambasted educators for neglecting the ends of the occupation and promulgating a grevious misconception of the nature of man. In Neo-Thomistic style, Maritain posited a twofold nature of man based on reason and Revelation:

> Thus the fact remains that the complete and integral idea of man which is the prerequisite of education can only be a philosophical and religious idea of man. I say philosophical, because this idea pertains to the nature or essence of man; I say religious, because of the existential status of this human nature in relation to God and the special gifts and trials and vocation involved.[32]

Maritain readily conceded the presence of many different religious concepts of man clarifying that his own perspective was a Greek, Jewish and Christian admixture. This view postulates that man is an animal endowed with reason whose supreme dignity is in the intellect; yet man is a free individual in personal relation with God whose supreme rightousness consists in voluntarily obeying the law of God. Maritain lamented that Robert Hutchins did not go far enough in his metaphysical enunciations because he did not take into account the facts about man and his destiny made known to him through Revelation. Without this acknowledgement, according to another Neo-Thomist, Thomas McGuckin, metaphysics has no base, no roots. Thus to quote Acquinas as Hutchins does without taking cognizance of the additions he made to Aristotle's thought is to quote an Acquinas who never existed. Without reference to Acquinas' thoughts on Revelation there is no Acquinas.[33]

The educational implications of the Neo-Thomist stance are that a wholistic concept of man can be derived only by calling into play the totality of man's powers - moral, intellectual and physical - by and for their individual and social uses, directed towards the union of these activities with their Creator as their final end.[34] For the Neo-Thomists, traditional education implied doing the job right - assuring a liberal curriculum and an appeal to all of the student's powers.

13

# VOCATIONAL/PRACTICAL EDUCATION

A third stream of educational thought and practice emerged in North America at the time of its industrialization. It was a time when leaders in business and industry looked to the schools as important suppliers for a specialized labour force. They believed that education founded on the classics was hopelessly obsolete in a modern industrial age. They were concerned about the mass of students who would not go beyond minimal literacy training and never become scholars. Was there a place in the nation for their energies and, if so, in what ways could they best be prepared for the non-scholarly role?

In Canada, the vocational movement began with the efforts of James L. Hughes and John Seath. The latter's interest in "manual training", as the theme was known, came about in 1889 when he visited systems of secondary education in some of the principal cities of the eastern United States. These schools were separate from the academic schools in the system, an arrangement which appealed to Seath and which he advocated in three subsequent reports to the Ontario Department of Education. Like Hughes, Seath was affected by the Industrial Revolution which he saw as providing an opportunity to a country that was prepared to educate their youth in a way that would maximize their potentialities. By 1911 Ontario had a new Conservative Government which quickly passed the Whitney's Industrial Education Act and prepared the way for Ontario's economy to make the shift[35] from an agricultural economy to an industrial base. Hughes, who was also involved with the advancement of manual training, promoted it on the grounds that it allowed for the total education of the student. Like the Neo-Thomists who argued for spiritual input, Hughes claimed that manual training took cognizance of a forgotten element in the child's development. Always the Froebelian (Wilhelm Froebel was the founder of the kindergarten system in Germany), Hughes saw manual training as a natural followup to the play activities of the kindergarten and as the starting point for other kinds of development.[36]

## One or Two Systems

The classicists sought to disallow the implementation of vocational schools in American education because they regarded such programs as noneducational in every sense. The progressivists were of various minds on the subject, although John Dewey did make a clear stand on the question early in his career. The central debate raged about the

14

question as to whether or not schools designed to prepare students for the job market should be incorporated into traditional systems. One critic of the two-system concept, Frank Tracy Carleton, voiced opposition to the "factory stage" kind of education whereby children would be processed by educational machinery to fit predetermined slots in a mass-produced system.[37] David Snedden, on the other hand, felt it to be a happy coincidence that human beings could be sorted by ability levels parallelling the hierarchical work requirements of modern society. This way citizenry could be fitted into the place they would eventually occupy in society by virtue of their abilities by previous groundwork provided via schooling. He suggested that the first few elementary grades should be the deciding levels at which such differentiation should begin.[38] Dewey countered this claim pointing out that the question of industrial education is fraught with consequences for the future of equality and democracy. He argued that if one system were maintained, democracy would be honored, but a two systems approach would accentuate undemocratic forces already at work in the schools.[39] In 1917, the USA Federal Government passed the Smith-Hughes Act which provided funding for a national system of vocational education administered through a separate Federal Board. It was the first and most important piece of federal legislation in the field of vocational education and its major provisions remained untouched for almost half a century to come.

The Cult of Efficiency

Raymond Callahan has described the movement toward a scientific measurement of educational failures or successes as the "Great Panacea", using the dollar as an educational criterion.[40] According to Callahan, the prelude of time leading to the passing of the Smith-Hughes Act was also the period in which America discovered the efficiency expert. In a sudden flood of enthusiasm with the notion, an attempt was made to apply the principles of scientific management to many aspects of American life. Of course, the school immediately became a target, and in 1911 a group of seven administrators were appointed to a committee on the economy of time in education. The name of Frederick W. Taylor vaulted into prominence via his book, Principles of Scientific Management, which was translated into many foreign languages giving sure indication that the concern for efficiency was not merely a North American phenomenon.[41]

It was Frank Spaulding, a superintendent of schools in Passaic, New Jersey, who popularized both the language and concept of efficiency, equating the education of children to

15

such physical and technical tasks as laying bricks, mining pig iron or cutting metals. The data on which he expected to base his measurement of a school's efficiency would include the percentage of children of each year of age in a respective school district, the average number of days attended for each child, the average length of time required for each child to master a sample concept or unit of work, and the percentage of children who actually completed a certain number of units. Ultimately Spaulding could come up with figures which indicated that a pupil recitation in English could cost 7.2 cents in a vocational school while it costs only five cents in a technical school. "Why are paying we a higher percentage of cost for the same skills in vocational schools than in technical schools?" he wanted to know.[42]

While classicists generally ignored these kinds of analyses and promulgations since they had nothing to do with real education anyway, the progressivists were appalled at the arrogance in relegating human tasks to the cognitive junk-heap of scrap metals and coal mines. The human mind was deserving of more respect than that, they claimed, and they severely castigated the efficiency promoters of disregarding individuality, creativity and the reality of individual perception.

## The Psychology of Efficiency

Taylor and Spaulding's principles of efficiency found ready support in the work of Edward L. Thorndike who developed a description of human learning in terms of the S R Bond concept and tried to show that the process is the result of the organism (human being) responding to a series of stimuli. He identified a series of inherited tendencies such as reflexes and instincts, differentiating them from learned acts such as those of skill or complicated acts of thought. Learning then becomes a matter of strengthening and weakening the bonds between a situation present to sense and responses in the nervous system, and the status of the response agent (person). The correct responses become fixed by exercise and the resulting satisfaction, while the unsuccessful responses are dulled or eliminated by virtue of the dissatisfaction which they engender.[43] In actuality, Thorndike's model was much more complicated than that, since he had to make allowances for circumstances in which the theory appeared not to work satisfactorily. Boyd Bode, however, criticized it as being nothing more than a combination of the[44] principles of the laws of readiness, exercise and effect.[44]

16

The blend of Thorndike's psychology and the cult of efficiency was quite functional in essence and objective. Thorndike once observed that education of the future would demand an increase in specialization and thus in the study of skills, habits, ideas and attitudes.[45] He was no doubt prepared to project laws by which these could be attained and Spaulding was prepared to measure their attainment by students (or should we say, by the organisms!). B.F. Skinner later carried on the behaviorist tradition by explaining away any concepts not previously dealt with by Thorndike. In analyzing human freedom, for example, Skinner may be accused of ignoring what has been said about existential freedom over the last one hundred years (i.e. the writings of Friedrich Nietsche, Soren Kierkegaard, Martin Heidegger and Jean Paul Sartre), and elaborating a scientific kind of concept, to wit: "Freedom is a matter of contingencies of reinforcement, not of the feelings the contingencies generate."[46]

The philosophical debate of the test-oriented followers of Thorndike with the progressivists continues to this day albeit in somewhat less headline grabbing ways. Among many educators there is a "both are right" attitude that prevails which gives evidence either to the fact of ignorance that prevails in that constituency or to the possibility that philosophical consistency is either an unknown or disvalued commodity today.

## Sputnik I, 1957

In the fall of 1957 the Russians launched the world's first mechanical satellite into orbit and the American scientific community went wild! Why were they not the first to accomplish this feat? Perhaps it was . . . yes indeed, it was because the schools had gone soft on learning and they were capable of excelling in the arena of scientific accomplishment. Progressivist ideas were blamed for watering down content and the classicists were slammed for emphasizing irrelevant ideas. Ivan could read and Johnny could not. Public education had become a wasteland of "experience-centred nothingness".[47]

Chief among the critics was the German-educated missile expert, Werner von Braun, who later guided the American foray into space, and Admiral Hyman Rickover, father of the nuclear-submarine program. It was almost comical to witness how quickly public funds could be allocated for "scientific" programs involving education from elementary through university levels. Anything even smacking of science was funded; teachers flocked to scholarship-sponsored summer schools and enrolled in a wide variety of institutes for course work that would allegedly improve their scientific orientation and expertise.

Putting the situation quite bluntly, critic Rickover charged that America was weak and becoming increasingly dependent on other nations who were becoming the "sinews of our economic and military power".[48] He found it paradoxical that Soviet engineers could do highly competent work despite authoritarian control and attributed their success to a contradiction in the Russian system. Apparently, they allowed some of their superior personalities special "capitalist-like" privileges. For America, the solution lay with the schools. Too many children were "enjoying" school but not getting the kind of education that the twentieth century required.

Part of the solution to the dilemma described by Rickover came in the form of the "Conant Report to Interested Citizens" authored by James B. Conant who served as United States Ambassador to the Federal Republic of West Germany from 1955-57. In the preface to the report, John W. Gardner, a strong Rickover supporter, commended Conant for his fresh look at the American education system, denied that Conant had been influenced by the Sputnik happening and encouraged Americans to accept Conant's challenge that any school could become a good school if his recommendations were implemented. Conant basically postulated the formation of a comprehensive high school system in the U.S.A. that would incorporate a variety of curriculum offerings, but particularly such that would challenge the most able students and thus build a pool of learned people in the nation. He argued that it was possible to provide a general education for all pupils to prepare them for their role as future citizens of a democracy and provide elective programs for the majority to develop useful skills, and educate adequately those with a talent for handling advanced scientific subjects.[49] Truly, it was to be a system with something for everyone.

The presses that hurriedly ground out several editions of Conant's Report had hardly cooled when the decade of the sixties began. It was a time of intrigue in American educational history, as many will recall, and initiated a series of alternative solutions, some of which were not even remotely connected to the three streams of traditionalism, progressivism or vocationalism.

Several social factors contributed to the development of the "I gotta be me" theme of the sixties. The Vietnam War was questioned by those who were enlisted to fight in it, the phenomenon of the flower children flourished, and there was a new social conscience emerged featuring concern for the poor, urban decay, exploitation of natural resources, and racial discrimination. Names like John Goodlad, Paul Goodman, Ivan Illich, Ashley Montagu, A.S. Neill, Jonathan Kozol, George Leonard, Myron Lieberman, and Charles Silberman dominated the educational scene.

Montagu borrowed from anthropology to make the point that a more humanistic atmosphere in the school would enhance learning.[50] Improved interpersonal relations as a means of producing more effective learning environments were also stressed by George Leonard. "Learning should be a sheer delight," he implored, "and is, in fact, life's ultimate purpose."[51] Later studies further developed this theme to incorporate concerns about adequate self-image as a foundation for enjoyable and effective learning.

Myron Lieberman took off after the professional and managerial aspects of schooling to make the point that significant changes were needed in the institution,[52] and John Goodlad articulated the concept of the ungraded school (continuous progress) as a form of internal reorganization[53] and later formulated principles for the development of "effective schools", i.e. increased student motivation, improved teacher morale, effective use of classroom time, etc.[54]

Charles Silberman demanded less change to the school as such, insisting instead that present curricula and process may be amended in ways so that students may actually enjoy school. Silberman analyzed past criticisms of schooling and suggested that the mindless self-fulfilling prophecies that dominate the institution could be replaced by an informal atmosphere of purpose. He advocated a new educational theme; one that builds on student awareness of the trust placed in them to guide the affairs of the nation and their schooling is a preparation towards that end. This combination projects both freedom and responsibility and avoids the dull routine of present schooling.[55]

It is difficult to formulate a comprehensive analysis of the educational reforms posed by the various writers because of the diversity of their perspectives. Illich and Reimer, for example, advocated closing down schools while Goodman liked much of what he saw in American education and merely postulated alternatives to the present setup, e.g. having no school at all for a <u>few</u> classes, dispensing with the school building for a few classes, eliminating compulsory class attendance, decentralizing urban schools and using a pro rate part of the school money to send children to economically marginal farms for a couple of months of each year.[56]

The following excerpts further illustrate the range of perspectives:

<u>Martin Buber</u>: Yet there are some I-Thou <u>relationships</u> which in their nature may not unfold to full maturity if they are to persist in that nature. . . I have characterized the relationship of the genuine educator to his pupil as being a relationship of this kind. In order to help the realization of the best potentialities in the pupil's life, the teacher must really <u>mean</u> him as the definite person he is in his potentiality. . .[57]

<u>Edgar Z. Friedenberg</u>: In high school, then, is where you really learn what it means to be a minor.[58]

<u>Herbert Kohl and Roland S. Barth</u>: Our schools are crazy. They do not serve the interests of adults and they do not serve the interests of young people. They teach "objective knowledge and its corollary, obedience to authority."[59]

<u>Jonathan Kozol</u>: School and media possess a productive monopoly upon the imagination of the child . . . Indoctrinational schooling and the mandatory practice of a twelve year house arrest are the keystone of a mighty archway in this nation.[60]

<u>John Holt</u>: Children are subject peoples. School for them is a kind of jail.[61]

<u>Ivan Illich</u>: I want to distinguish my aim to de-school society from objectives of other critics of the school system to seek either to transform the world into a classroom or to establish free schools, independent of the system.[62]

<u>A.S. Neill</u>: Education must be geared to the

psychic needs and capacities of the child. . . The extensive disciplining of children is harmful and thwarts sound psychic development.[63]

Neil Postman and Charles Weingartner: School, after all, is the one institution that is inflicted on everybody, and what happens in school makes a difference - for good or ill. We use the word "inflicted" because we believe that the way schools are currently conducted does very little, and quite probably nothing, to enhance our chances of mutual survival. . .[64]

Everett Reimer: Effective alternatives to schools cannot occur without other widespread changes in society. But there is no point in waiting for other changes to bring about a change in education. . . . Educational change . . . will bring fundamental social changes in its wake.[65]

One common strain in the "radical" literature on education in the sixties is that they wanted schools to change, even though there was little argument as to the direction for that change. In some instances, as in the case of the plea for an enhanced social conscience, there was some consensus.

## Education with Social Conscience

In 1979 Neil Postman pronounced the era of school reform in America over. With forty-five million students to educate in ninety thousand schools, under the supervision of roughly two million teachers, there was considerable resistance. In reflecting on the decade of the sixties with some degree of melancholy, Postman admitted that his own views had since taken on more of a conservative tack. He now offers the conclusion that the revolution failed because many of the reformers lacked a sufficient understanding of the complexity of the school as a social institution. Many of them were utopians, with a strong contempt for teachers and administrators and lacked an official connection to the school itself. Now, with a seventeenth-century glass-blowing display drawing just as large a crowd as a school reform session, serious school criticism is barely alive.[66] Postman, like many of his formerly zealous would-be changers of the school, is tired; he merely wants to preserve the rudiments of traditional schooling.

Postman too easily disregards some of the lasting

21

campaigns of the sixties motivated by such individuals as Robert Havighurst, Christopher Jencks and Paulo Freire. Freire is a Brazilian educator who labored vigorously to teach minimal literacy to the peasants of Brazil with a minimum investment of time and facilities. Schooling as an institution could never accomplish what Freire did with his foray into the marketplace, contending that only the oppressed can free themselves and their oppressors through reflective action.[67] Jencks offers a more localized version of the same philosophy and has shown that educational research has debunked a number of popular myths like poverty being hereditary, the notion that rich people have better cognitive skills or that school reform can substantially reduce the extent of cognitive inequality. He argues for a revamping of public policy to match the reality of life in America fast moving toward the equalitarian perspective.[68] Havighurst has lambasted the educational critics who have nothing positive to say about the promising changes to schooling and has launched his own campaign to foster self-concept building as a major theme in areas where minority peoples reside, as a means of encouraging better educational results on the part of their children. Included in his package is the teaching of minority history and culture as a means of fostering better personal outlooks on life.[69] Much of Havighurst's work has been incorporated into multicultural programs in schools all across North America.

As the pendulum of educational change continues to swing, albeit with a less vigorous beat, several mandatory features of schooling need to be reiterated and underscored. Foremost is the need continually to formulate and clarify the philosophy of education which serves as the tiller for educational process and change. This is a fundamental component often ignored or overlooked. Second, is a recognition of the tendency to mold schooling according to some perceived social need, depending on the strength of influence of a particular lobbyist group. Schooling deserves better than that. Third, is the need to foster the continuing fundamentals of learning, i.e. curriculum and methodology and the fulfillment of pupils' needs and expectations. Finally, there is the matter of what are often perceived to be the more extraneous features, e.g. school management and the professional status of teachers. Regardless of social mood or the nature of proposed reforms, these components remain as vital to the very existence and basic functions of our educational institutions.

# REFORM RECOVERY

The pedagogical world heaved a sigh of relief when the sixties were over so much that the next decade was essentially a pulling back from reform and a quest for pedagogical sanity. It did not occur to the "back to the basics" promoters of the seventies that the school had emerged from the onslaught of the previous ten years virtually unscathed. Of course, there were vestigates of radicalism to be observed, i.e. a few free schools lingered into the next decade and the home schooling movement gained converts, but generally speaking the ideals of the bandwagon of "return to the fundamentals "occupied the minds of most school trustees and parents and even some educators. In Alberta, the Premier of the province entered the scene with a call for an undergirding of "the new basics" although these were never defined either by the Premier or the Ministry of Education

With reform recovery well underway by the nineteen eighties, educators have concentrated on refinements to the system. These include a few carry-overs from the previous decade along with several innovations, i.e. community schools, effective schools, continuous progress, cooperative education, multicultural education and peace education. Private schooling has also expanded, perhaps as an expression of disillusionment with public education. No one seems to know what to do about public education any more, and if the reforms proposed in the past have failed, there is not much hope for success on the horizon. A careful analysis will also reveal that the philosophical presuppositions underlying many of the "new" proposals are basically minor modifications of the progressivist movement, i.e. cooperative education, multicultural education and peace education.

Many observers have wondered aloud why the reforms of the past have been so ineffectual. There are still classes to attend, lessons to be learned, exams to be written and non-academic events to be supervised. With few exceptions in schools where special smoking areas are provided, even the facilities look the way they did fifty years ago. What, if anything, has changed? The answer is that such assessment, if any is undertaken by educators, will be lost in the challenge of yet another social concern, this time motivated by technological considerations. If it is true that the implications of the microchip when fully developed will make the Industrial Revolution look like a hiccup of history, we indeed stand on the verge of yet another educational onslaught. The battle for control of the schools will take

23

another twist; technology proponents will vie for the attention of young people to learn the language and appreciate the concepts of the new phenomenon. School budgets will reflect purchases of the new technology, and the nation's youth will need to be appraised of the extent to which subsequent changes will affect everything from daily patterns of thinking to international trade. The revolution has already begun, but the inevitability and desirability of technological life is never raised as an issue. The facts of planning, qualifications, systematization of control and management by technical expertise are taken to be "fixed" - as givens.[70] And the role of the school has not clearly been defined.

## Still Another Dimension

The bulk of educational reform proposals have bypassed the teaching profession per se except for such occasional diatribes against teachers as those launched by Lieberman[71] or Neatby[72] who appear to hold teachers personally responsible for education's ills. Other authors, like Ulich[73], MacKinnon[74] and Koerner[75], recognize the perplexities encountered by the profession in trying to meet the socialization expectations foisted upon it and their lack of political power. None of these writers, however, appear to have considered formulating an educational reorganization that would acknowledge the potential of teachers and better advance their professional requirements. Everyone readily recognizes that the last generation of teachers views itself and is viewed by the public as worthy of greater professional status and respect[76], but little has been done either by the community or by the profession itself to remedy the situation. Certainly, the format of having the policies for their professional conduct and performance set by outside groups such as school trustees and politicians deserves a hard look. It is a subject which will be taken up in more detail in later chapters, and a solution will be posed. Some educational challenges, like this one, do not require a massive overhauling of either philosophical outlook or administrative structure; in many ways, they merely require common sense.

## FOOTNOTES

[1]Ernest E. Bayles and Bruce L. Hood, Growth of American Educational Thought and Practice, New York: Harper and Row, 1966, 222.

[2]John Dewey, "The School and Society", in Martin S.

24

Dworkin, Ed., Dewey on Education, Selections, New York: Columbia Teachers College, 1964, 50-51.

[3]For further discussion, see Ernest E. Bayles, Pragmatism in Education, New York: Harper and Row, 1966, chaps. 2 and 3.

[4]Robert Ulich, Crisis and Hope in American Education, New York: Atherton Press, 1966, ·64-65.

[5]Charles E. Phillips, The Quance Lectures in Canadian Education, Toronto: Gage, 1955, 88.

[6]Lawrence A. Cremin, The Transformation of the School, New York: Random House, 1961, 243.

[7]W.R. Wees, Nobody Can Teach Anyone Anything, Toronto: Doubleday, 1971, 49.

[8]W.R. Wees, The Way Ahead, Lectures delivered under the Quance Lectures in Canadian Education, Toronto: W.J. Gage, 1967, 45.

[9]Ibid., 195.

[10]C.A. Bowers, The Progressive Educator and the Depression: The Radical Years, New York: Random House, 1969, 98.

[11]George S. Counts, "Dare the School Build a New Social Order", in The Teacher and the Taught, by Ronald Gross, New York: Dell, 1963, 178-193.

[12]Theodore H. Brameld, Education as Power, New York: Holt, Rinehart and Winston, 1965, 103, quoted in Christopher J. Lucas, Foundations of Education, Englewood Cliffs, N.J.: Prentice-Hall, 1984, 384.

[13]For background information on the work of individual Canadian educators, see Robert S. Patterson, et.al., Profiles of Canadian Educators, Toronto: D.C. Heath, 1974.

[14]Arthur E. Bestor, Educational Wastelands, Urbana: The University of Illinois Press, 1953.

[15]Ibid., 11.

[16]Max Rafferty, What Are They Doing To Your Children?

New York: The New American Library, 1963, 11-18, quoted in Contemporary Critics of Education, edited by Howard Ozman, Danville, Ill.: Interstate Printers, 1970.

[17]Max Rafferty, American Education, 1975-2000", in The Future of Education, 1975-2000, edited by Theodore W. Hipple, Pacific Palisades, Calif.: Goodyear Publishing Co., 1974, 160-180.

[18]Max Rafferty, What Are They Doing To Your Children? New York: New American Library, 1963, 43.

[19]James D. Koerner, The Miseducation of American Teachers, Boston, Mass.: Houghton-Mifflin, 1963, 1-10.

[20]Frank MacKinnon, The Politics of Education, Toronto: University of Toronto Press, 1962.

[21]Hilda Neatby, So Little For The Mind, Toronto: Clarke, Irwin, 1953.

[22]Mortimer Adler, "In Defence of the Philosophy of Education", The Forty-First Yearbook of the National Society for the Study of Education, Part I, Philosophy of Education, edited by Nelson B. Henry, Chicago: University of Chicago Press, 1942, 197-250.

[23]Mortimer Adler, How to Read a Book, New York: Simon and Schuster, 1940.

[24]Mortimer J. Adler and Peter Wolff, A General Introduction to the Great Books and to a Liberal Education, Chicago: Encyclopedia Britannica, 1959, v-vi.

[25]Robert M. Hutchins, The Conflict in Education, New York: Harper and Row, 1953, 69.

[26]Robert M. Hutchins, Education for Freedom, Baton Rouge, Lo.: Louisiana State University Press, 1943, 26.

[27]Mortimer J. Adler, "The Future of Democracy: A Swan Song", in Humanistic Education and Western Civilization, edited by Arthur A. Cohen, New York: Holt, Rinehart, 1964, 30-43.

[28]Jerome S. Bruner, The Process of Education, New York: Vintage Books, 1963.

[29]Allan C. Ornstein and W. Eugene Hedley, Analyses of

Contemporary Education, New York: Thomas Crowell, 1973, 271.

[30] Jerome S. Bruner, Toward A Theory of Instruction, Cambridge, Mass.: The Belknap Press, 1966, 5.

[31] Jacques Maritain, Education at the Crossroads, New Haven: Yale University Press, 1943, 6.

[32] Ibid., 7

[33] William McGuckin, "The Philosophy of Catholic Education", in The Forty First Yearbook of the N.S.S.E., 251-288.

[34] Ibid., 255.

[35] R.M. Stamp, "John Seath: Advocate of Vocational Preparation", in Robert S. Paterson, et.al., Profiles of Canadian Educators, 233-254.

[36] R.M. Stamp, "James L. Hughes: Proponent of the New Education", in Ibid., 192-214.

[37] Quoted in Christopher Lucas, Foundations of Education, Englewood Cliffs, N.J.: Prentice-Hall, 1984, 168.

[38] Ibid., 169.

[39] Ibid., 170

[40] Raymond Callahan, Education and the Cult of Efficiency, Chicago: University of Chicago Press, 1962.

[41] Ibid., 22-23.

[42] Ibid., 74.

[43] V.T. Thayer, Formative Ideas in American Education, New York: Dodd Mead and Co., 1965. See Chapter 10, "Education as Adjustment: Edward L. Thorndike and the Psychology of Behaviorism", 213-242.

[44] Boyd H. Bode, Modern Educational Theories, New York: Vintage Books, 1927, 178-179.

[45] Edward L. Thorndike and Arthur I. Gates, "The Ultimate Aims of Education", in Readings in the Philosophy of Education, by John Martin Rich, second edition, Belmont,

Calif.: Wadsworth, 1972, 23-33.

[46] Quoted in C.A. Bowers, Cultural Literacy for Freedom, Eugene, Oregon: Elan Publishers, 1974, 158-159.

[47] Christopher Lucas, Foundations of Education, 10.

[48] H.G. Rickover, Education and Freedom, New York: E.P. Dutton, 1960, see Chapter One.

[49] James B. Conant, The American High School Today, New York: McGraw-Hill, 1959, xi-xiii.

[50] Ashley Montagu, Education and Human Relations, New York: Grove Press, 1958.

[51] George B. Leonard, Education and Ecstasy, New York: Dell, 1968.

[52] Myron Lieberman, The Future of Public Education, Chicago. University of Chicago Press, 1960.

[53] John I. Goodlad, "The Nongraded School", in Crucial Issues in Education, edited by Henry Ehlers, fourth edition, New York: Holt, Rinehart and Winston, 1969, 279-282.

[54] John I. Goodlad, A Place Called School, New York: McGraw-Hill, 1984.

[55] Charles E. Silberman, "Crisis in the Classroom", in Analysis of Contemporary Education, edited by Allan C. Ornstein and W. Eugene Hedley, 292-317.

[56] Paul Goodman, Compulsory Mis-education, New York: Horizon Press, 19-42.

[57] Martin Buber, I and Thou, quoted in Howard Ozman, Contemporary Critics of Education, 45-50.

[58] Edgar Z. Friedenberg, "Coming of Age in America" in Innovations in Education, edited by John Martin Rich, Boston: Allyn and Bacon, 1975, 62-68.

[59] Herbert R. Kohl and Roland S. Barth, "So You Want to Change to an Open Classroom" in Critical Issues in Education, fifth edition, edited by Henry Ehlers, New York: Holt, Rinehart, 1973, 232-239.

[60] Jonathan Kozol, "Look, This System is not Working",

in The Radical Papers, edited by Harold W. Sobel and Arthur W. Salz, New York: Harper and Row, 1972, 50-51.

[61]John Holt, "How Children Fail", in Analyses of Contemporary Education, edited by Allan C. Ornstein and W. Eugene Hedley, 50-82.

[62]Ivan Illich, "The Deschooling of Society" in Alternatives in Education, edited by Bruce Rusk, Toronto: General Publishing, 1971, 103-126.

[63]A.S. Neill, Summerhill: A Radical Approach to Child Rearing, New York: Hart Publishing, 1960, xiii.

[64]Neil Postman and Charles Weingartner, Teaching as a Subversive Activity, New York: Dell, 1969, xiii.

[65]Everett Reimer, "An Essay on Alternatives in Education", in The Radical Papers, edited by Harold W. Sobel and Arthur E. Salz, 154-179.

[66]Neil Postman, Teaching ss a Conserving Activity, New York: Delacorte Press, 1979.

[67]Paulo Freire, "Pedagogy of the Oppressed", in Innovations in Education, edited by John Martin Rich, 187-193.

[68]Christopher Jencks and others, "The Schools and Equal Opportunity", in Crucial Issues in Education, edited by Henry Ehlers, 41-47.

[69]Robert J. Havighurst, "Requirements for a Valid New Criticism", in Challenges to Education, edited by Emanuel Hurwitz, Jr. and Charles A. Tesconi, Jr., New York: Dodd, Mead and Co., 1973, 540-556.

[70]Christopher Lucas, Foundations of Education, 18.

[71]Myron Lieberman, The Future of Public Education.

[72]Hilda Neatby, So Little for the Mind.

[73]Robert Ulich, Crisis and Hope in American Education.

[74]Frank MacKinnon, The Politics of Education.

[75]James D.Koerner, The Miseducation of American Teachers.

[76]In a 1953 study by the Canadian Education Association it was discovered that teachers viewed requirements for academic training much lower for teachers than business or industry did. No doubt today's teachers are not as easily satisfied with their preparational requirements nor status. See Paul Nash, "Quality and Equality in Canadian Education", in Canadian Education and Ideology: Readings by John W. Friesen, Lexington, Mass.: Xerox, 1975, 3-12.

Chapter Two

REFORM AND CHANGE:  FOR BETTER OR WORSE?

Institutional reform is often as ineffective as
rearranging the deck chairs on the Titanic
- anonymous

To suggest that North American schools are a
diminished, hollowed institution as commonplace as apple pie.
Reports are rampant about drug abuse, violence, and
alcoholism; of teacher burn-out, disappointed parents and
resentful taxpayers.[1]   Additional complaints pertain to
declining test scores, outdated teaching methods and the
perpetuation of a whole host of so-called frills that serve only
to contaminate the real purpose of public schooling.

We are living in a period of turmoil insofar as the
function of social institutions is concerned, marked by a
discontinuity with the past, anxiety about the present and
uncertainty about the future.[2]   Right now, of course, no one
really seems to know what the purposes of our basic social
institutions are or what form they may take in the days
ahead.   Thus, "anything goes" insofar as criticism is
concerned.   School systems specifically tend to function
better in periods of economic calm when the prospects of a
bright future are visible;  they do not hold up well to unjust
criticism or when attacks on them are based purely on
economic considerations.

Society has a tendency of analyzing institutions during
tough economic times and the current assault on schooling is
certainly no exception.   Familiar criticisms are being stepped
up, for example, with regard to the high costs of schooling,
the literacy question, teacher competence and school
management.   Each of these charges has an element of
justification, of course, but of itself is hardly of the
magnitude to threaten civilization or constitute an undue
expense on the taxpayer's shoulders.   If we simply consider
the advantages of public schooling, it is easy to conclude that
the institution is basically a boon to society, not a burden.

This is not to say that "all is well" in public education,
for that is surely not the case.   Changes do need to be made
in many areas but imagination to do so is often severely
lacking in quarters where responsibility lies.   The purpose of
this discussion is to indicate several possible solutions to one
particular problem of schooling, namely, its format and
management, with a view to whetting the appetite for major
reform.   Each of the proposals discussed here is intended to

furnish direction for possible change and is not intended as a panacea. In fact, the nature of at least two of the proposals presented later is such that a closer look at the implications should be enough to startle any caring educator or parent. Still, they need to be examined because they are being proposed by individuals in the public sector.

## Finances: The Big Question

The first cry to go up in an economy fraught with capital shortages (often emanating from government overspending) is "where can we cut back?" Public institutions are frequently easy targets to consider, although schooling is an exceptional case in that those who govern its ongoings are not the people who labor on the firing line. School trustees, in other words, find it easier to make cut-backs than officials in other publicly operated organizations because of the traditional gap that has been perpetuated between teachers and trustees.

Possibly the greatest honeymoon for public schooling was in the late fifties when the Sputnik event brought attention to the potentiality of schooling to make America into a great scientific nation. "How could the Soviets get so far ahead of us," was the question raised, and politicians and educators sprang into action. The result was beefed up curricula, expanded facilities, more rigorous teacher training, and new scientific equipment.[3] Today's outcry against public education has a similar ring to it. We aren't getting enough for our dollar. Kids can't read as well as they should. Our education budget is too high.

Beyond a doubt, expenses for public schooling have risen a great deal in recent years. The cost of elementary and secondary education in the U.S.A. has gone from 15.9 billion in 1960 to 100.1 billion in 1980. The cost per American citizen is $450 per person or $749 per taxpayer. Canadian statistics are similar with the Province of Alberta, for example, claiming that 22% of total government spending in 1982 was for educational purposes. Reasons advanced by educators to explain upwardly spiraling costs include added "frills" like daycare, breakfast and lunch programs for disadvantaged pupils, and a whole array of special services for mentally and physically handicapped. No one likes to attack the nature of these extra expenses or even those that result from attempts to modernize schooling, i.e. purchase of computers or other ways to meet public expectations. A desperate Minister of Education in Alberta recently suggested that the school had better forget about fulfilling the duties of

other institutions like the family and the church and
concentrate on educational obligations.

Despite rising costs it is well to note that there are at
least a few defenders of public education and one of them is
John R. Bormuth of the University of Chicago. He claims
that literacy, which is the primary function of schools, pays
off - big. By including the costs of producing and
distributing literacy materials and the cost of teaching people
to read and write, Bormuth calculated the costs of public
schooling in 1976 to be $285 per person. By estimating the
ratio of benefit to cost, Bormuth calculated that every dollar
invested in public education produced about six dollars in
national income.[4]

There are other advantages to public schooling besides
economic considerations which may be called social outcomes.
The results are not always conclusive, but there are some
indications that schooling has positive effects in terms of
reducing prejudice and discrimination among pupils. There
are also impressive correlations between the amount of
education acquired and employment figures. This also holds
true for the factors of lack of education and time spent in
prisons.

Generalizations about the advantages of public education
are not convincing to those who are out for the blood of the
school. "Enough is enough" is the slogan of the day;
apparently, the explanation about the relationship between
expensive education and positive social effects is not
satisfactory. Claims like those made by John Egerton that
"there has never been a time when larger numbers or
percentages of young people have completed the requirements
of schooling, left with a greater and more diverse store of
knowledge, or went on to advanced training in such a
multitude of endeavors"[5] are simply not wanted at this time.
Some citizens are simply "fightin' mad!"

A few educators appear willing to take a share of the
blame. John H. Holcomb, a superintendent in Lamar,
Colorado, suggests that public schools have gotten themselves
into a bind. He states:

> First, we have not defined our product, and
> second, we have not confined our activities to
> developing that product. For education, whether
> we want to admit it or not, is a product. And it is
> our product. We can define education, measure it,
> determine who is doing his job and who is not.[6]

Not every professional would be willing to admit that education can as easily be categorized as Holcomb does in terms of it's marketable characteristics. To admit that creates problems on two fronts: it intimates that what is essentially a human process may be assessed on technical grounds and it encourages evaluations of educational procedures by those who consider themselves consumers. In both instances the human element is sold short on it's affective characteristics and inclinations so that the picture becomes distorted.

Educational reform is at least partially a financial matter, though it's philosophical concerns are of more significance. Questions that need to be settled even before further money is spent or structures are reorganized are these: what do we want children to know as a result of their having attended school? What attitudes do we want them to have? What is the best method by which children can be taught? What resources are we willing to commit to public education? Who shall govern or control our schools? When these questions have been settled we can begin to restructure schooling. At that point even finances may not constitute the foremost priority.

The Literacy Debate

"Why Johnny Can't Read" is a headline that has been around for at least a decade, ever since someone decided that schools were falling down on the job of promoting literacy effectively. A related conclusion is that North American colleges are helping to spawn a generation of semi-literates, as evidenced by the fact that even the best colleges have a significant number of graduates who cannot pass a written communication test. A few years ago, at the University of Berkeley, where students come from the upper 12.5 percent of high school graduates, nearly half of the freshman class was required to take a course in remedial English in order to qualify for university work. Similar statistics are available from many other North American universities.

College and university personnel have been reluctant in accepting criticism of their lack of success in the literacy function and many of them have simply referred the blame to the nations' high schools. Educators at that level have tried to divert the accusation by pointing out that schooling today is concerned with a much greater responsibility than the three "R's", i.e. responsibilities pertaining to family life education, driver education, consumer education, and a whole host of others. A related defense is that knowledge is accumulating at such a vast speed today that it is difficult to acquaint students with such developments while maintaining a high standard of skill attainment.

Evidence against the school's success in promoting literacy is not clear-cut, and much can be said on the other side of the argument. First is the matter of success in reaching the populace. Today more than ninety percent of America's adult population attends public school, thus assuring prominence in such fields as worldwide communications, science, technology, electronics, medicine and even sports. In fact, the United States produced the first man on the moon even during a time when criticism of this nature was mounting. Few countries can boast as high a literacy rate as Canada and the United States, and when comparisons are made, that literacy standard is probably higher than that of most other countries agitating for the cause. Recent studies utilizing standardized tests reveal that today's elementary children fare better than their counterparts in the nineteen sixties, for example.[8]

What is to be made of this jungle of figures and studies concerning literacy? Can we be sure that all of the evidence is in when we condemn schooling? How do the following facts fit into the picture? In the United States in 1950, ten percent of black students admitted graduated from high school. In 1977 that rate rose to seventy-six percent. Even if literacy is of an inferior quality, and no one responsible is admitting that it is, perhaps even the experience of graduating from high school is a positive factor in the life of a minority member of society. In 1910, the average 25 year-old American had completed 8.1 years of formal schooling. In 1950, that figure rose to 9.3 years and in 1975 it was up to 12.3.

There are also statistics available to indicate that schooling is productive on other counts than literacy. Besides keeping youngsters in school and graduating them, the "functional literacy rate" in the United States has dropped from 11.3 percent in 1900 to 1.2 percent in 1970. Reading scores on both comprehension and vocabulary have increased steadily over the first three grades of schooling of the past decade. As Donald Thomas, Salt Lake City's superintendent of schools suggests, "it is time for someone to defend this tower of education from shipbuilders, newspaper columnists and college-circuit speakers. The public schools of the nation have served us well."[9]

Good service notwithstanding, few institutions can serve

so well that they cannot be improved. And while the evidence either for or against the school is not conclusive, there may still be a need to make innovative changes in the school, if even better service can be provided.

## The Private versus Public choice

One of the more popular reactions to public schooling's failure has been the development of private schools. In some states and provinces there has been considerable support for them, financially and in other ways, but for many educators the choice is not an easy one.

Recently, a national controversy originated in the United States over the appearance of the James S. Coleman report entitled, "Public and Private Schools". Many people worried that Coleman would defend the record of private schools in the U.S.A. and thus encourage such ventures as tuition tax credits and vouchers which would only serve to undermine public schooling. Coleman did conclude that private schools (Catholic specifically) did more nearly proximate the American ideal, but he shied away from making policy recommendations that would encourage further development of the private system. Essentially, Coleman may be credited with making a neutral but important statement on education. Schools do make a difference.[10] Corollary claims are that school achievement emanates not from a particular family background but from specific school policies. He discovered that private high schools produce better achievement than public high schools, not because they are private but because they "create higher rates of engagement in academic activities."[11] School attendance is better, students do more homework, and generally involve themselves in more academic disciplines. One important difference he noted was the extent of curricular tracking. Only thirty-four percent of public secondary students were enrolled in an academic curriculum, while thirty-nine percent were in a general curriculum and twenty-seven percent in vocational. By contrast, seventy percent of those in private schools were in academic programs, twenty-one percent in a general program and nine percent in vocational.[12] It is the emphasis in school that makes the difference in output rather than the compiled characteristics of the students who attend. More than anything, however, Coleman underscored the importance of education and stressed the potential power of educators to dramatically influence a child's life chances.

A few critics of private schools mince no words in their opposition. Laurier LaPierre, for example, said recently that

36

he believed private schools breed snobs, are an instrument for abusing children, and they are more concerned about a parent's image than the child's.[13] LaPierre had recently completed a two-year study on schooling when he made his observations and based his remarks on the assumption that public education has been unduly harshly criticised and private education has been allowed to get away with unorthodox activities.

Denis P. Doyle points out that private schooling is on the rise in America, although the reasons for growth are unclear. Until 1971, public school enrollments had grown steadily, even dramatically, but in 1972 for the first time in memory, public school enrollments declined.[14] Private schools, on the other hand, decreased in enrollment during the 1960s and 1970s but reversed the trend in 1974. Anyone can guess as to reasons for this trend, but the best evidence points to more disposable income for educational spending and a general disillusionment with public schooling. In Canada, the proportion of all pupils attending private schools fluctuated very little for the nation as a whole from 1920 to 1978, and a decrease after that date may be attributed almost solely to the Province of Quebec where a drastic reduction in the number of private schools occurred in 1978 - 1,705 in 1959-60 to 797 in 1977-78.[15] In other provinces, private schools have grown, spawned mainly by religious organizations such as Mennonites, Adventists and Christian Reformed. Bergen suggests that disillusionment with public education is probably not the predominant reason for private school growth as much as it is the fact that public schools cannot accommodate the unique educational emphasis that religious groups desire. Proponents of private schools, like other citizens, pay taxes and vote. The solution to the possible disintegration of public schooling as we know it, Bergen suggests, is for public school authorities, whether at provincial (state) or federal levels, not merely to oppose or actively retard private school developments, but rather work out appropriate controls and even symbiotic arrangements.

Some of the more frequently raised claims for privatizing schooling is that they are more successful in the academic realm. When the roster of enrolled students is examined, however, it may be found that their characteristics are also atypical. Often students from higher income families gravitate to private schools, mainly because their parents are better able to afford it. Staff members at these schools often take unusual pride in their work to the extent that they boast of an intensified degree of professional integrity and independence. Other reasons include a better environment, physically and socially, manageable size of plant and system, a program that is tailored to the needs of students, staff and constituency, moral emphasis or at least "value-centred" curriculum, and mutually satisfactory peer-group contacts.[16] In contrast to most public schools then, one would have to conclude that the private school pupil has decided advantages.

In determining the extent to which private schools should be financed, two significant questions must be raised. The first is that private schools traditionally have catered to an exclusive social strata in society. Private schools, it is claimed, segregate different segments of the population, due to the "self-selective" character of the schools. They draw the economically affluent from the public system and then engage in economic stratification resulting in a form of elitism. They are also accused of segregating racially by drawing off students of W.A.S.P. background, leaving children of minorities to occupy public schools in larger proportion. Even more basic than these concerns, however, is the postulation that to encourage private schools financially in any way is to violate the separation of church and state principal that is fundamental to the American way of life.[17] The last accusation is based on the easily supported supposition that most private schools have religious connections, which they do, but it grossly ignores the history of schooling in Canada which is virtually the reverse of that of the United States. In Canada, every school system founded in the days of the birth of the nation had religious origins. In addition, the maintenance of a separate religious system or systems in the various provinces is a clear repudiation of the contention that all North America heeds strongly the notion of separation of church and state.

As a matter of historical record, public schooling in the United States actually emerged in the nineteenth century and by the beginning of the twentieth, became available to every American child. By making schooling compulsory, however, two additional tendencies developed. Private schools emerged to serve those who for one reason or another did not like what they found in the public sector, and ethnic and religious groups pursued the freedom often broadcast in the nation and developed their own forms of schooling. Not everyone welcomed Horace Mann's educational philosophy, and not everyone relished the essentially protestant system that was promulgated as a public entity. As time passed many people forgot about the religious origins of American schooling and began to assume that only private schools had religious connections.[18]

The resolution of the public-private argument will have to deal with five realities identified by Chester E. Finn, Jr. The first is that governmental financial resources for additional funding are drying up. These are tough times, and in such times, programs are cut and only those activities that are labelled important are funded. Secondly, the world of the private school is not that of a unified community. Ideally, one should be able to conceive of a public system of education and, if a second is originated, it should encompass the "desired alternatives". Nothing could be further from reality, however, because of the diversity among the various private schools and systems to say nothing of the skepticism and mistrust with which such schools view each other. Third is the overwhelming realization that a significant proportion of the general public regards private schooling with suspicion. Somehow, they are different, perhaps even involved in an activity that is not in keeping with the basic objectives of the nation. No one can easily put their finger on what that disparity with common values might be, but many are convinced that it exists. In this instance, the old adage about "fear of the unknown" appears to prevail. Fourth is Finn's contention that private schools have never really enjoyed the wholehearted support of the various elites that essentially determine the direction of the American nation. Major private foundations, the elite universities, editorial pages of many metropolitan newspapers and the most prestigious "think-tanks" and research institutes do not generally hold private schools in the same regards as they do say private universities, private hospitals or private libraries. Finally, despite having implied a great deal against the successful persistence of private schooling, Finn acknowledges that such institutions are still in reasonably sound economic shape. None of the systems have a particularly high surplus of resources, but they are faring well.[19]

Finn contends that support for private education will likely continue, and they may even become the recipients of further funding from public sources. The first of his observations along these lines is to suggest that private education's vitality will be assured by subsidizing them with something resembling unrestricted revenues. The argument that they serve at least a segment of the body politic will produce the corollary claim that they have a right to a portion of the public purse as well. Parallel with this assumption is the concept that nothing should be taken from private schools they now have. In other words, if benefits are maintained or even intensified, no additional requirements or regulations should be required of them. Third, Finn postulates that a campaign will be mounted by supporters of private schools claiming that they have been denied benefits which they rightfully deserve as citizens, and they will bargain publicly for distributive justice. The specific manifestations of these claims may run the gamut from highly specific to quite vague. He contends that supporters of private schools will use the following arguments in promoting their case: parents bear the principal responsibility for the upbringing and education of their children and should thus be offered a choice in the type of school sought; well-to-do families already have such a choice due to the financial format of existing private schools (which are usually too expensive for lower income families) so that option should be made available through choice in a publicly-supported system; and, since America is a heterogeneous combination of nations (both Canada and the United States), it will be claimed that such a format virtually dictates the necessity of offering choices. The familiar theme of mediocrity emanating from government operations will also be raised. The implication is, of course, that if schools are decentralized to the extent that local boards can recognize diversity through private schooling, inefficiency and monopolization will be reduced. Tax credits and the formation of a voucher system are perhaps[20] the best known of proposed systems in this regard.

An appropriate concern about private schools has to do with the exclusivity they allegedly foster either by catering to a special interest group or by emphasizing a philosophy of education, which may be at least a little out of step with the value system of dominant society. Of course, all liberal-minded educators will concur with the postulation that diversity makes for interest, but there may still be other considerations. Some critics feel that all educational organizations, including public and private schools, should be allowed to bid on an open competitive market for both clientele and financial resources.[21] The obvious problem is that there would be nothing to stop each educational institution from establishing entirely unique standards for curriculum and teaching credentials so much, perhaps, that radical differences might emerge. These differences might be easy to justify from a theoretical perspective, but the crunch could come when it would be discovered that children from a few exceptional schools might be cheated of literacy, warped by a values frame that mitigates against equality for all citizens or shortchanged in some other pedagogical way.

The tough question to face is the matter of interfering in the democratic rights of citizens while at the same time guaranteeing such for the nation's young. Canadian education has experimented for some years with the format of alternative schools within public systems, and the practice of providing funding to private schools has similarly been a long-established practice in some provinces. British Columbia, for example, started off by providing the sum of $500 per pupil per year in 1979. Alberta offered to pay up to seventy-five percent of operating costs for private schools and Manitoba gradually shifted its policies so that private schooling could also be aided. Specifically, the alternative plan took effect so that by 1983 in Calgary, Alberta, the public system had three different kinds of alternative schools within its system: Jewish, Christian, and the Plains Indians Cultural Survival School. When a new school board was elected in the fall of 1983, the Jewish and Christian schools were eliminated on religious grounds. It was argued that to maintain them within the public system was somehow a violation of democratic rights.

In essence the alternative school arrangement offers the best of many worlds. It allows for the formation of schools with diverse philosophies, yet can guarantee such essential components as a standardized curriculum, assured levels of literacy and certified, pedagogically competent teachers. It is a format worthy of pursuit, theoretically and functionally. Restructuring schooling to acknowledge diversity may take some educating on the part of educators and politicians responsible, and, as will be pointed out later, it is only one of several fronts requiring explanation and defence against public bias.

The Question of Teacher Competence

A parallel social process to public school criticism is the national pastime of "teacher bashing". Some journalists, like Phil Keisling of the Washington Monthly, are blunt in their appraisal: ". . . the quality of our schools has plummeted. The lion's share of the blame must fall on the nation's 2.2 million teachers."[22]

Criticizing teachers today is a much less credible sport than it was a few decades ago because of the strides taken by faculties of education to better prepare teachers for the classroom. The standard four-year degree is giving way to an even longer term of preparation and many North American teachers already have graduate degrees as well. It may be argued that preparation per se is no guarantee for quality performance, but it must be borne in mind that the same universities that are responsible for teacher education also

41

train personnel for other professions which are often free of criticism insofar as quality is concerned. It is singularly ridiculous to assume that only one faculty in each university, namely education, can function below par when others appear to be doing satisfactory work.

Blaming teachers for societal maladies is not without an element of logic, however, and in a sense Keisling is right when he points his finger at teachers because they <u>are</u> in the action pit of ailment. As the decades have rolled on, schools have become a convenient dumping ground for the socialization tasks abandoned by other institutions. After all, schools are supposed to provide basic education, aren't they, so why not make it complete? Thus, the curriculum has added to it items like consumer education, family life and sex education (where it is not opposed), driver education, values (and sometimes moral) instruction, and even concerns about world peace. As the education profession has taken on these additional responsibilities, the teacher's workload has increased. Strictly academic tasks can no longer be thoroughly treated because in essence teachers have become surrogate parents. Insofar as reinforcement is concerned, possibly the only time teachers hear from the community is when criticisms are voiced.

Tackling additional responsibilities has also taken its toll on teachers personally. Statistics will bear out the observation that as traditionally stable families have "paid the price" for a fast-changing society, so have those who serve in teaching, thus making it even more difficult for them to fulfill the role of pedagogical therapist.

We simply cannot expect the school or any other institution or profession by itself to cure all our social ills effectively. When all factors are taken into account, it is similarly unfair to blame a profession for trying to act as savior.

Keisling's diatribe against schooling is based on the assumption that the profession historically attracts the nation's least academically gifted and creative students. He also claims that the course of instruction for teacher preparation is stultifyingly dull.[23] Add to this the observation that the widespread sexism of a quarter century ago attracted many of the nation's housewives to a career readily open to them because of the parallel hours it offered to their children's absence from home, and you have an almost iron-clad case for condemning schooling wholesale.

Some educators in Canada are even more outspoken than Keisling.[24] A Canadian provincial publication, The Alberta Report,[24] recently implied that the number of competent teachers in the provincial system was high and blamed inadequate training, the tenure system, and professionals protecting their colleagues for the unfortunate situation. Citing a master's thesis completed by William Stockman, the publication goes on to suggest that even good teachers degenerate to incompetence because the job fosters burn-out due to no respite from pressure. Such teachers eventually resort to use of workbooks and handouts, thus shirking their teaching responsibilities because of a degenerating interest in the task and eventually slip away to other professions. A few hang on to early retirement.

The apparent cure for the burnt-out teacher, assuming that the phenomenon is either real or growing, is sabbaticals, retraining or career counselling for the troubled. As the economy continued its downswing, however, it is unlikely that much will be done and the malady will prevail. As such it will also be a contributing factor in fostering public misunderstanding and criticism of the profession.

Public opinion of the teacher profession is radically different from that of any other profession, since it is thought that teachers have a very personal responsibility, in relation to child development. In actuality, many other professions also labour within the realm of child psyche formation, i.e. social workers, counsellors and family case workers, pediatricians, etc. The format of schooling is in essence what causes the problem. So long as the responsibility for administering education remains in the hands of often uninformed albeit elected officials, the effectivity of the teaching profession will be severely hampered.

Assessing what constitutes professionalism varies little from one profession to another. As Powell puts it:

American educators, having embraced an uncritical faith in science and engineering early in the century, have expected high school teachers, at their best, to be like doctors. They should possess arcane technical skills and dispense treatments to somewhat passive clients. In contrast, what would be the implications for developing effective support systems for teachers if teaching were considered less a science or profession and more a calling or craft? What if one

43

emphasized qualities in teachers such as engagement, commitment, compassion, passion for a subject, genuine affection for youth, and the capacity to make wise educational judgments amidst uncertainty or conflicting expert opinion?[25]

We expect a unique attitude towards one's work; a theoretical rather than a technical orientation, consisting of the ability to apply theory to specific situations; possession of a body of systematic theory; rigorous selection (an area into which education is fast moving); acceptance and continued expansion of as many paraprofessional categories as there are technical services to be provided; self-employment, which allows services to be offered to the public on an individual basis, and withheld at the will of the professional organization as a whole, and a lengthy period of formal training in an acceptable university setting, a token of the cost of which was paid by the individual trainee.[26]

It is the second last criterion, that of self-employment, which keeps teachers from attaining full status as a profession. The fact that status matters in terms of job satisfaction, self-evaluation of work and even effectivity is borne out by many studies. Chapman and Lowther suggest that career satisfaction, for example, is enhanced through the criteria a teacher uses to judge his or her professional success, particularly with respect to job challenge and rewards. Also significant are professional accomplishments to date, with particular respect to job challenges and recognition by others.[27] Isherwood and Taylor, in their study of teacher participation in educational decision-making, found that teachers involved themselves in decision-making on the basis of four factors, the first of which was increased professionalism.[28] As teachers gain increasing control over the function entrusted to them by society, they appear to gain in proficiency as well.[29] Perhaps when schools become independently operated by professional educators, as one of the alternatives later outlines, society will witness an increased measure of production in such revered commodities as literacy, mathematical computation and scientific appreciation.

## The Fundamental Question

Perhaps the obvious question should have been raised at the outset of this discussion, but it may be as relevant here: "Do we really need public schools?" Virtually every civilization has adopted a form of introduction process for its young, whether it be a means whereby children could learn

44

adult roles in an informal setting or via the formalized school system as we know it. Some critics like Everett Reimer and Ivan Illich go so far as to suggest that we have paid greater tribute to public schooling than is really necessary. If the major objective of the enterprise is to promote literacy, for example, we do not really know if it can deliver. Close examination will show that there are always more literate members of a society than have gone to school and there are always children attending school who do not even learn to read. Generally speaking, children of literate parents learn to read even if they do not attend school, while children of illiterate parents fail to read even after attending school. Similarly, the reading diet of children whose parents are active in intellectual environments, e.g. university or college teaching, have a much more intense interest in books than the children of parents who do not even read the daily news.

When the data on business and everyday math are examined, it will be found that society's illiterates all seem to be able to count, add and subtract even if they never went very far in school. Only a small percentage of people in a fully schooled society ever learn much more or need much more. Achievement tests in mathematics indicate that only a few students do much better than chance in the formal structure of the subject. Students who are interested in mathematics do much better than those who are not so motivated. It would be hard to prove that the school can even stimulate an added interest in the subject.[30]

If these critics are right and public schooling is still in need of a defence there must be better reasons to argue for the preservation of the institution than on its record in promoting literacy and basic math skills. On the other hand, is the evidence that the goal of literacy has been short-changed sufficient reason to vote to close down public schools? What about other kinds of evidence? Johnson, for example, points out that there are some very good reasons to maintain schools as preventative institutions in terms of reducing some of society's ills. In other words, schooling can help reduce what are generally conceived of as unfortunate social situations; it can serve a preventative function.[31] Of course, there are conditions to be met if schooling is to be effective. For example, one cannot simply make statements about random relationships between school attendance and literacy in defence of schooling. It is helpful here to refer to a series of tested principles for attaining excellence through schooling researched and advocated by David Donovan. First, we know that the more time spent in instruction, the greater the achievement gain; the greater the parental involvement, the greater the achievement; high expectations from the principal are associated with greater achievement; high teacher expectations are associated with high achievement; higher achievement gains are more likely in classrooms with a high degree of structure and with supportive teachers; and, use of positive feedback or reinforcement by teachers is associated with greater achievement.[32]

Even more convincing than the evidence presented on behalf of effective schooling is the conviction of John Egerton who states, "Public education, for all its flaws and shortcomings, is the nearest thing we have to a publicly owned and operated institution devoted to the general welfare."[33] It may be dangerous to admit that schooling is basically a "socialist" agency, but in one sense it is and it needs to be. Preserving the public school is probably the only way to preserve equal opportunity, to assure equal access to learning to members of all economic echelons of society. Moreover, it is a leavening institution - children from various families, religions and subcultures meet to exchange ideas, to share with one another, to help form the next generation of our nation. According to Arthur Powell, "One of the better-kept secrets of American education is its historic commitment to serve the 'average' children, a commitment which contradicts the usual images of high achievement and academic elitism in private schools."[34] If the commitment to serve the "average" child is to be maintained, and if the general social obligation of schooling is to be fostered, the question about whether or not we need schools becomes secondary to the query, "What kind of schooling do we want?" Is it possible to ensure the basic principles of democratic, universal, compulsory, practical and comprehensive education while experimenting with new forms? Can a major reconstructuring of schooling occur and still avoid violating those rights that are central to North American life? The discussion in the following chapters will take up that challenge by offering a diversity of suggestions insofar as school renovations are concerned. An attempt will be made to provide sufficient fuel for cogitation so that if choices are finally made they will be accomplished on the grounds of having examined thoroughly a wide variety of alternatives. If schooling has played a significant role in creating the current conditions of social and economic progress we must be dedicated to maintaining and perhaps even enhancing that role. If we do not invest sufficient resources, financial as well as social, in schooling, it is conceivable that we will pay greater social costs later on.[35]

The inevitable path for all who are concerned with public schooling is to seek to pursue better education on democratically palatable grounds even if a major restructuring of a somewhat tired institution is required. That task, to be completed satisfactorily, will rely on an examination of those educational alternatives that mingle a concern for good education with a genuine appreciation for what is best for the nation's children. It is to a discussion and analysis of several such alternatives that we now turn our attention.

## FOOTNOTES

[1]Amitai Etzioni, "An Immodest Agenda: Rebuilding America Before the Twenty-first Century", excerpted in Learning, February 1983, 43-45.

[2]Norman Henchey, "The Future of Canadian Education", Education Canada, Winter 1981, 14-21.

[3]Christopher Johnson, "Our Investment in Public Education". Today's Education, February/March 1982, 14-17.

[4]Ibid.

[5]John Egerton, "Can We Save the Schools?" The Progressive, March, 1982, 26-28.

[6]John H. Holcomb, "The Public Wants its Schools Back". American Education, October 1982, 4-8.

[7]Ibid.

[8]Editorial, American School Board Journal, June 1980, 19-22.

[9]Ibid.

[10]Diane Ravitch, "The Meaning of the New Coleman Report". Phi Delta Kappan, June 1981, 718-720.

[11]Ibid.

[12]Ibid.

[13]Calgary Herald, Thursday, February 24, 1983, p.B7.

[14]Denis P. Doyle, "A Den of Inequity: Private Schools Reconsidered". American Education, October 1982, 11-18.

[15]John J. Bergen, "Private Schools in Canada". Education Digest, January 1982, 13-15.

[16]Denis P. Doyle, "Public and Private Education". Phi Delta Kappan, September 1980, 16-19.

[17]James S. Coleman, "Public Schools, Private Schools, and the Public Interest". American Education, January/February 1982, 17-22.

[18]Chester E. Finn, Jr. "Public Support for Private Education, Part I". American Education, May 1982, 4-9.

[19]Ibid.

[20]Chester E. Finn, Jr. "Public Support for Private Education, Part II". American Education, June 1982, 7-13.

[21]Donald A. Erickson, "Should All The Nation's Schools Compete for Clients and Support?" Phi Delta Kappan, September 1979, 14-17, 77.

[22]Phil Keisling, "How to Save the Public Schools". Education Digest, January 1983, 2-5.

[23]Ibid.

[24]Eric Reguly and Stephen Weatherbee, "When Teachers Are Terrible". Annual Report, January 31, 1983.

[25]Quoted in Pat Hutcheon Duffy, A Sociology of Canadian Education. Toronto: Van Nostrand and Reinhold, 1975, 128-129.

[26]David W. Chapman and Malcolm A. Lowther, "Teachers' Satisfaction with Teaching". Journal of Educational Research, Vol. 75, No. 4, March/April 1982, 241-247, italics mine.

[27]Arthur G. Powell, "Appreciating the Dualism of Public and Private Schools". Education Digest, May 1982, 11-13.

[28]Geoffrey B. Isherwood and Robert M. Taylor, "Participatory Decision-Making via School Councils". High School Journal, Vol. 61, No. 6 (March 1978), 255-270.

[29]John W. Friesen, et.al. The Teacher's Voice: A Study of Teacher Participation in Educational Decision-Making in Three Alberta Communities. Lanham, Md.: University

Press of America, 1983, 2-4.

[30]Everett Reimer, "An Essay on the Alternatives in Education". The Radical Papers, Harold W. Sobel and Arthur E. Salz (Eds.), New York: Harper and Row, 1972, 161.

[31]Christopher Johnson, "Our Investment in Public Education", 14-17.

[32]David L. Donovan, "Schools Do Make a Difference". Education Digest, January 1983, 28-29.

[33]John Egerton, "Can We Save the Schools?" 26-28.

[34]Arthur G. Powell, "Appreciating the Dualism of Public and Private Schools". 11-13.

[35]Christopher Johnson, "Our Investment in Public Education". 14-17.

## Chapter Three

## PROFESSIONALS AND NON-PROFESSIONALS:
## WHO'S IN CHARGE HERE?

A recent phenomenon in schools has been to increase the number of personnel working in the classroom besides teachers, and this includes paraprofessionals of several varieties as well as parents. The reasons for adding the energies of these groups to the dynamics of school functioning are varied and numerous; parents, for example, may have been challenged to spend more time assisting with the socialization process of their children as part of a "counter-attack" on the part of educators who feel the school has been taking too many such tasks from the home. The underlying rationale for getting parents back into the school has been based on the idea, "Its time you came to help us raise your children."

A parallel reason may also have originated with parents who have felt left out of the socialization process and who may begrudge teachers the time they can spend with their offspring and sought to get in on the action. No doubt some of the concern has been related to the notion of social values which the school is sometimes accused of transmitting erroneously or insufficiently, and parental involvement in the school is seen as a means of offsetting this.

In some instances a kind of "missionary" purpose is inherent in the trend to increase the number of paraprofessionals in the classroom, particularly with regard to children of different cultural background whose lifestyle and thought processes pose a tough challenge for the teacher who lacks training in multicultural education or in related skills. In such instances, teacher aides or paraprofessionals of the same background as the pupils have helped to interpret cultural habits and language to the teacher. This is true particularly with regard to situations where English is taught as a second language and where paraprofessionals have special knowledge and/or abilities that will assist the teacher. Assigning paraprofessional tasks to handicapped persons has also occurred in some situations and the rationale has been that such a program may give jobs to those who need them and who would not otherwise be employed.

Financial concerns are never far away from the educational scene and the question of hiring paraprofessional help is no exception. In some school districts school aides have even been engaged to replace teachers because their services could be obtained at less cost and yet they could legitimately perform many of the non-teaching tasks expected of teachers. For politicians and do-gooders concerned with providing literacy skills to lower socio-economic areas of the country it has also become reasonable to do this at as low a cost as possible. This view may not necessarily be described as one that takes cognizance of the many different components of a well-rounded program of education, because basic literacy is seen as the singular challenge of education. When it can be provided at a reduced cost this should be done. Any success in such a program makes good telling when constituents are particularly concerned about rising costs.

Not least on the list of reasons for the emergence of the paraprofessional concept in education is the idea that the teachers' workload of responsibility in the area of non-professional tasks can be reduced by the assistance of a trained teacher aide. Sometimes the idea has worked, but there are also professional considerations pertaining to the function of a non-certified person working in direct contact with the pupil. If teacher training delivers what it purports to, namely any individuals who are truly professional in the sense of being informed in knowledge, method and human relations, the matter is certainly worthy of further examination. Additional help, strange as it may sound, under some circumstances may actually produce more problems than benefits.

The uninitiated may think that paraprofessionals make a teacher's job easier. They do not; they should not. It is true that the duties of the paraprofessional will release the teacher to initiate activities at a higher and broader professional level and a better learning environment may even result. However, the arrangement may also take its toll in terms of requiring management skills on the part of the teacher which he/she may not have, and may also introduce a new factor into the function of the classroom, i.e. discipline problems may arise.[1]

The promotion of the paraprofessional concept has been undertaken by many different organizations and in varying contexts. All promoters of the idea are pledged to "serve the school" and eager to lend their assistance. If the laboratory of learning gets any more crowded than it is, however, we may even have to consider the elimination of either teachers or students from the classrooms of the nation.

Welcome to our Schools

As early as 1914 in Canada, Loren De Wolfe of Nova
Scotia had urged teachers to form Parent-Teacher groups in
their communities, and when the Canadian National Federation
of Home and School was formed in Toronto in 1927, De Wolfe
set about bringing a chapter into being in his home province.
Eight years later there were 166 associations in Nova Scotia[2].
At first the organization concentrated on such activities as
enlarging school grounds, obtaining play equipment,
providing hot lunches and buying books for the school
library. Their meetings were essentially social times,
bringing parents and teachers together to discuss and to
celebrate their common interests. Usually a newsletter was
published to enhance communication or to highlight special
concerns.

At present, PTA groups have adopted a wider range of
objectives than those originally incepted and these include:

1. The promotion of the welfare of children and youth
   in home, school, church and community.
2. Raising the standards of home life.
3. Securing adequate laws for the care and protection
   of children and youth.
4. Seeking to bring the home and school into closer
   relation so that parents and teachers may cooperate
   intelligently in the training of the child.
5. Developing between educators and the general
   public such united efforts as will secure for every
   child the highest advantages in physical, mental,
   and spiritual education.[3]

Despite the many advantages of PTA groups, their
activities often represent another source to draw energy from
the teacher and their efforts may even interfere with the
administrative operations of the school. Still the movement
has grown, partially fuelled, perhaps, by individuals who
believed the school to be insufficiently sensitive to the needs
of their children.

One of the more radical books on schooling and written
from a nineteen sixties perspective is by Ellen Lurie entitled,
How To Change The Schools.[4] Drawing on her involvements
in the local PTA of Washington Heights in New York, Lurie
concluded that the school was bad. Along with a few dozen
colleagues she organized a letter campaign, set up a volunteer
after-school reading centre, fought for smaller classes,
additional guidance staff and secretarial help and remedial

help. With each complaint and subsequent innovation she discovered that the bureaucracy of the school became better organized to offset her concerns. She concluded that the school system did not really care about children and continued to stifle them, manipulate, correct and adjust them to suit the objectives of the system. Thus she determined to write a manual for parents on how to infiltrate the system and bend it to the needs of children and the wants of parents. Provocative chapter titles include: How to make a school visit, How to recruit and hire good teachers, How to evaluate and upgrade your school staff, How to get rid of a truly terrible principal, What to do if your child is suspended from school, etc. Obviously, Lurie was concerned only with parents' rights, and scarcely recommended anything that would diminish the harmful and traditional concept of the adversarial nature of teacher-parent contact. Her rules for effective parent-teacher conferences indicate this. She suggests that these conferences be arranged at the parents' convenience (after all, parents are working people), a baby-sitting service should be provided by other teachers if the parent brings other children along, and the teacher should provide detailed information about the child's progress, health and attendance information and anecdotal information.[5]

Echoing a similar but milder tone, Robert Stamp, in a book published in 1975, About Schools: What Every Canadian Parent Should Know[6], lamented that parents did not have sufficient access to schools. Except for community schools which were just coming into being in Canada about that time, he described the typical experience of a parent to witness "welcome" signs such as "Visitors please report to office" on arrival at the school for a visit. Stamp suggested that parental rights should be honored at schools including access to their legal, medical and psychological files as well and outlined a series of rights which had not yet been established, namely, the right to educational choice (alternative schools), representation on a wide variety of school committees, and access to an ombudsman in the event of failure to have a complaint properly attended to. At the risk of coming down on the side of the latest educational fad, Stamp outlined several problems of incorporating parental input into the school beginning with the observation that the nature of that output will vary widely from one community to another. He argued that no general outline or manual of activity for parents may be prepared, for in some communities parents may be totally immune to the idea of participating in school decision-making or activity. The bottom line is that when an apathetic audience has been challenged to increase their involvement and they refuse to do so, they should be allowed the privilege of choosing non-involvement. Many parents are simply of the opinion that schools have a task to do in the same way that any other professional institution manages itself and they can utilize the services of that institution on any basis they choose. They may even find newsletters or phone calls from the school annoying. Few commentators of this period were as generous as Stamp.

Perhaps the most serious concern about increased parental (or community) involvement in schools stems from professional considerations. Will teachers be interested in additional input from parents? Are they prepared (trained) for it? Will there be enough time in the day to attend to classes plus accommodate the concerns of another outside group? In the struggle for power that so frequently erupts as a result of this situation, how can both sides be appeased or accommodated? Must they, in fact, appear as sides?

Stamp suggests that teachers often complain that parent organizations may be suspect, perhaps because of the nature of participation they frequently vie for. Teachers sometimes think that a parent's interests alone do not qualify him to decide educational policies. After all, would a parent's interest in a child's health qualify him to perform a surgical operation?

Parental involvement in schooling may not only fail to mesh with teacher operations but they can also run the danger of subverting or negating any attempt at broader educational policy-making at the municipal, provincial or national levels. Having a group of community leaders suddenly decide what is good for their community without seeking to coordinate their efforts with the overall policy or plan of the larger school system may actually be dysfunctional even to the envisaged goals of the would-be reformers.

Nothing that has been said above is intended to give the impression that parental or community involvement in schools is either undesirable or nonproductive. What needs to be accomplished, however, is the development of a proper format and procedure for such input so that the professional domain of the teacher is not hampered and student learning and social development is maximized.

## Formalizing Community Input

An effective way of incorporating parental concerns in the school has been to develop "Parent Advisory Councils" which may be called on to offer input for special occasions. These councils have proven useful in many school districts in relation to matters of instruction, curriculum, community acceptance of the school program, and the development of new courses of study. Frequently, their members have been appointed by the principal on nomination by classroom teachers or by the district superintendent or the board of education. The arrangement has served to offset possible community tensions about school operations and, on the positive side, helped to develop a healthier respect for education. In some of the United States it is even a mandatory requirement, especially where federal funds are involved.[8] The movement to inaugurate parent advisory councils was originally part of the American Head Start, Follow-Through and Title I programs, and soon spread to other school districts as well. Often touted as part of the "citizen participation movement" in the U.S.A., advocates of the idea are now agitating for a part in the decision-making process that has to do with "... how money is being spent, making sure the curriculum correlates with what the children will be doing in the future, and the hiring and firing of teachers and administrators."[9] The future will reveal what kind of a balance may be worked out between citizens (parents) and teachers insofar as such factors as control and participation in decision-making are concerned.

One of the fastest growing school emphases in the nineteen seventies is the community school movement which accentuates the objective of utilizing school staff and facilities for total community use. Some proponents have articulated the concept of a twenty-four hour program" implying that many activities will be added to the existing school program. Other objectives include: providing the community with additional information about the school, securing community support for school programs, developing programs employing community resources and meeting the expressed needs of community constituents. The original mover for community schools was the Mott Foundation of Flint, Michigan, which made funds available for these purposes.

Some of the highlights of community school programs include additional involvement of parents in school programs, increased activities and responsibilities for school staff, and an intense inter-agency cooperation with service clubs, churches, and government offices etc. in the community. Some of the activities that have resulted include the production of a community newspaper, more frequent consultation with community people as resource persons, and health, drug, craft and other classes and programs for interested residents. Community schools require additional funding, of course, and their increased agenda have brought parent advisory committees into being to supervise and evaluate the direction and nature of these activities.

Increasing the offerings of the school is generally viewed as a very positive development with promises to provide a place for teenagers to "hang out" after hours, provide elderly people with social opportunities, and give full use to school facilities as some have suggested, "to get our money's worth out of the schools." The requirements for an effective program are obvious, however, and consist basically of time and money. In addition, it is often difficult to get the various agencies who might be helpful to cooperate on a program - school boards think they own the building, principals think they should be in charge, and teachers are reluctant to become involved in an already crowded after-school schedule. It is perfectly plausible to envisage increased parental involvement in a school program but unless these areas of concern and responsibility are carefully worked out, the program may do nothing more than add to an already heavy workload for teaching staff and administration.

A positive feature about community schools is that their formation has greatly enhanced parent interest in the education of their children. At the same time it has triggered a belief on the part of many participants that schools would function better if they were managed by the community. Some have even gone so far as to suggest that the goals of education had been lost in the rising bureaucratic shuffle that represents the growth of schooling,[10] and only the community can bring them back. The resultant sharing of the workload, however, has not always been clearly defined so that the new party can function in the school setting on amicable terms with those who have traditionally held that responsibility. With the traditional arrangement established over the decades of the functioning of public schooling, the onslaught of a group of enthusiastic but inexperienced and untrained community volunteers could create quite a challenge for school administrators. Community school proponents argue that before they organized themselves, school input by laymen was limited to peripheral and ceremonial functions of education. Parents and students had basic rights insofar as choice was concerned, but these[11] did not extend to management of school affairs. Some educators also preferred to have it so that any advisory input from community sources could also be considered only as advisory - they could heed it if they wanted to or ignore it.

A second significant educational movement that has increased community involvement in schools is the "Effective Schools Project" which was encouraged by such writers as John Goodlad[12] and Ronald Edmonds.[13] Essentially, the program is based on the following principles:

1. Our schools are presently effective and this is a program that builds upon our strengths.
2. Schools are unique social cultures and as such are constantly growing and developing in response to internal and external forces.
3. It is the school which should determine its direction and how to get there.
4. The school requires a common philosophical base upon which to make its decisions and to plan for the professional development of its members.
5. School decisions can now be based upon significant educational studies.
6. Schools which develop cross-subject and cross-grade decision-making groups will find that the resultant consistency leads to a more positive ethos.
7. Effective teaching is better facilitated in a school which has consciously developed a positive ethos based upon consistency and high expectations.
8. The effective school program is only one way that schools can build upon their strengths and determine their direction.[14]

Goodlad sees the school as a facility "where it all comes together", and the place to engage in a collaborative process of improvement. This requires active participation on the part of administration, teachers, parents, pupils and other affected community personnel. Goodlad's research has revealed that there are seven particular factors that make for effective schools. These are:

1. Use of rewards and praise.
2. Emphasis on learning.
3. The level of expectations that teacher behavior represents.
4. Student participation.
5. Appearance and comfort of school environment.
6. School organization and teacher skills.
7. Firm leadership and teacher involvement in decision-making.

The manner in which the above factors are operationalized in the local school will depend on the route selected by the people in that particular setting. The staff, parents and students of one such school, Ian Bazalgette Junior High School in Calgary, for example, decided to approach the matter by spelling out the meaning of each statement in terms of their own school and developing a series of action statements they would follow in bringing the statement to reality. In terms of rewards and praise they established such activities as: sending students to a writing workshop, sponsoring a spring fair featuring student work, developing a reward and praise booklet, featuring a "student of the week", and developing a "warm fuzzy" award system. Staff members are provided with a supply of "warm fuzzies" to give to their students whenever they feel their use would be effective. The program also applies to colleagues.[15]

Obviously the E.S.P. requires a great deal of additional work on the part of school staff and administration. Many hours are spent working with advisory and implementation groups which include parent and student representatives. These participants have felt right at home with the program often volunteering much extra time to make it work. When the Parents Advisory Committee was asked to evaluate the project they had high praise for the school staff but wondered just how long they could carry on such a heavy workload. As one parent put it, "The only fear I have is teacher burn-out." When it was suggested that the principal might leave the school for this reason one parent stated, "We would want to know where he is going so we could send our kids there."[16] Clearly, one of the guarantees to making the program work is to demand extra effort on the part of school staff and administration. How much more work they can absorb in addition to an already full schedule will remain to be seen. The question also has to be raised as to the manner in which school staff are recruited for the project; is there any element of coercion involved?

It will be tempting to wipe aside any possible criticisms of the E.S.P. because of the overwhelming advantages. According to the Ian Bazalgette experience, these include:

"-    a dramatic increase in staff and student morale
 -    a marked change from concentration on crisis discipline to concentration on instructional improvement
 -    a greater staff and student consciousness of the importance of success and achievement
 -    an increased sharing of successful classroom techniques and strategies
 -    an increase in scores on in-school and system-wide

tests
- a dramatic decrease in school vandalism
- a decrease in student and staff absenteeism
- a more positive approach by the staff toward problem-solving
- a decrease in staff transfers
- an increase in library use and book circulation
- an increase in awareness of how individual efforts fit into the total school plan
- an increase in student, teacher and parent cooperation."[17]

It is difficult to argue against these successes except to say that the evidence is not yet all in. A three year period of experiment is probably not sufficient to judge whether or not the novelty of a new approach will wear off. Research on E.S.P. generally is also of fairly recent duration and can offer guidance on a somewhat limited basis.

The increase in adjunct assistance to school staff is often thought to be of recent origin because of such innovations as community schools and the Effective Schools Project. There are several such movements, however, that predate these programs by quite some time. One of them, in fact, The Lancaster Method, was at least an eighteenth century idea.

## The Lancaster Method

It is probably not common knowledge that the alleged founder of this plan did not invent it at all. Although two people, Joseph Lancaster and Andrew Bell are credited with originating the idea in 1798, there is evidence to suggest that its germ was at least three hundred years in the making. Winchester College and many other British schools had a form of the plan in operation long before Lancaster created his version. Briefly stated, the monitorial system consisted of the teacher instructing a number of brighter pupils who in turn taught other groups of children. These students (monitors) were also responsible for such tasks as keeping order, checking attendance and other details of school routine.[18] It was the first case of the use of paraprofessionals in a teaching capacity in the Western world.

In 1804, Lancaster began lecturing about his teaching abilities in caring for up to 1,000 pupils and still demonstrating literacy results. Essentially based on a rewards concept, Lancaster believed that a spirit of competitiveness among students guaranteed motivation, and he therefore ranked the pupils (boys only) in his class according to their successes on achievement tests. When a boy did well he was awarded a badge which would remain his if he could maintain his achievement in the next level of the school program. If he retained the badge for two lessons he was awarded a picture he could keep permanently.

Lancaster believed that schooling could function at a much cheaper rate than it had previously and to prove this he emphasized the procuration of inexpensive materials - slates, books and chalk. He also employed a sand-box which was substituted for other materials and an exercise might proceed as follows: the boy with the highest merit badge would begin by writing with a stick in the sand for a particular demonstration and the rest of the class would follow according to rank. A similar approach was used for the teaching of reading and the development of math skills.[19]

In 1809 the monitorial system was formally approved in the United States by the Governor of New York. Over the next decade many American schools experimented with the method to fit their own requirements - Philadelphia, Boston, and in the South. It prospered in England until the early 1850s but was gradually criticized by the church. At first it was seen as a good idea for the teaching of the Scriptures, but later church leaders worried about inaccurate denominational interpretations that might be fostered. They were also concerned that the power of the church might be undermined by an enlightened lower class. What resulted was the development of a counter school system headed by the National Society for Promoting the Education of the Poor in the Principles established by the Church throughout England and Wales. Lancaster's supporters formed the British Foreign School Society and waged a battle to dominate British education. Both systems eventually waned because of the heated controversy and other factors such as the emergence[20] of an awareness of professionalism on the part of teachers. The American decline was partially motivated because of opposition of the factory mentality of the schools and on grounds that "the republic deserves better". The argument was that the automatons produced by the factory system were incapable of running a republic, and the monitors were being deprived of their own educational advancement by functioning as servants of the teacher in the classroom.

Paraprofessionals and Teacher Aides

In 1953 the paraprofessional movement as we know it got underway in the Bay City School System in California,

60

motivated by a study which concluded that teachers spend up to 69% of their time on non-instructional tasks.[21] The result was that any teacher with more than forty-five students was provided with the services of a college trained teacher aide who worked much like the monitors in the Lancaster model. These individuals were not allowed to teach but served in menial functions under the direction of a certified teacher. The arrangement was intended to provide the teacher with more instructional time and generally proved to be a satisfactory concept.

In 1965 it was Title I of the Elementary and Secondary Education Act that provided seventy-five million dollars for a new careers program and piggybacked on the developments in paraprofessional education in the earlier decade. A simultaneous emphasis on individualized instruction in American education also sparked curiosity in the paraprofessional concept and brought about a resurgence of interest in the area. Inner city schools were targeted as primarily in need of such assistance and the result was not only an increase in the number of people thusly employed but an enhancement of their tasks to include some "borderline" teaching tasks.

The growth of the contemporary paraprofessional movement included three essential elements in its American beginnings. First, it was intended to relieve the professional teacher of menial work; second, it was to foster community involvement; and third, it was aimed at communities where low literacy levels could be identified and alleviated through increased pedagogical attention. Teachers greatly appreciated the opportunity to spend more time on planning, diagnosing problems and prescribing courses of action to be taken, but as time developed they also began to resent the increasing control (or rapport) which some aides gained over their students. Professional teacher organizations also began to balk at the notion of uncertified personnel in the classroom who might work in diversionary ways against the teacher's goals.

It is helpful to note that the paraprofessional phenomenon is not unique to education, and many professions have had to struggle with the challenge of working with less qualified and uncertified help - nursing, law, mental health workers, dentistry, and medical staff, for example, and in each case the solution to effective functioning has had to be worked out in unique terms. Former Saskatchewan Premier Allan Blakeney once suggested that lawyers would need to expand their delivery team if they were going to handle the increasing case loads society is casting upon them. He envisaged that paraprofessionals who could handle much of the paper work at a lower cost would help to keep legal fees affordable for citizens.[22] In medicine the role of the paramedic has increased to the extent that they are frequently seen as bridging the gap between community and hospital because of the many personal kinds of tasks they perform at the practical level. Some studies indicate that the effectiveness of the paraprofessional is beyond question with the majority of patients contacted for information offering support for their role. In some cases, chronically-ill patients have even declared a greater degree of help from paraprofessionals than they have received from professionals. This impression may rightly be gained from situations where professionals have simply been too busy to spend the time with the patient that he or she would have desired. It is precisely for that reason that the job of the paraprofessional was created.

Do we need all this help?

The role of the paraprofessional is rapidly expanding on many fronts and for very good reason. An increase in teacher services which means more help is needed is a definite factor, but it must also be emphasized that the complexity and technology of each profession is demanding an increasing amount of time merely for the individual to keep up with developments in his profession. Some professions are now instituting systems whereby constant upgrading is required for an individual to maintain his or her status within the profession. New techniques and research findings are rapidly changing the shape of many traditional practices with the result that anyone not keeping abreast of new developments may fall behind rapidly. In teaching specifically, there has been a significant increase in the kinds of tasks and responsibilities that have been assigned (or taken up) by the school. This has enlarged the teacher workload in many "unprofessional" areas which could be carried out by someone with less training in the field, perhaps none (how many degrees do you need to help a first-grader on with his rubbers?) At the same time, the working relationship of the teacher and the paraprofessional need to be clearly elucidated. At what point and under what conditions is an aide assigned to a teacher? Does the teacher have any say in the matter?

The economics of the paraprofessional phenomenon are also relevant here. Most programs involving the use of aides in the classroom in the United States have been financed federally. This is because their inception has been justified on the basis of "extraordinary need", something which is usually outside the scope of state responsibility. However, the cutbacks that are currently underway in every sphere of social services in America will likely affect education severely because it is this sector that employs more paraprofessionals than any other human service.[23]

The origins of the paraprofessional function in Canada emerged largely in the area of Native education. Here the aide was usually a Native person skilled in the language of the community in which the school was located, and his/her task would be to interpret what the demands of the school were to the child. The aide would also act as interpreter, particularly in instances where the behavior of the child was not readily understood by the teacher. In the nineteen sixties, when the movement began, it was usually the case that teachers working in Native communities were rarely Native and frequently unaware of the workings of Native culture. Often they were immigrants to Canada and unfamiliar even with the nature of culture in Canada generally. Thus a very complex set of circumstances faced them in teaching Native children and the Native aide was frequently considered a godsend.

Perhaps the most popular employment of the aide's time has been with regard to individualized instruction, but this is also where controversy has erupted. A child who has difficulty reading might find it easier to approach the aide because of familiarity with the Native language. This is to be expected but when this has happened the ire of teacher organizations has been raised and teachers have even felt threatened because of loss of rapport with the student. In the Northwest Territories, for example, there are 140 classroom assistants in sixty scattered communities, some of them with more than ten years experience and most of them quite enthusiastic about improving their academic qualifications. A Special Committee on Education established in 1980 made recommendations about the continued use of teacher aides in the classroom, suggesting that three different levels be established: assistant teacher, associate teacher and teacher intern. An assistant teacher would be selected by the local education authority and must demonstrate a desire to work with children. He or she would then work under the supervision of a trained teacher and become fluent in the primary language of instruction. Another requirement would be to follow a program of study that is the equivalent of one year of academic study which could be spread over two summers and two winter training sessions.

On completion of this course of study the assistant teacher becomes an associate teacher. Although associate teachers may remain at their level, working under the supervision of certified teachers, they may also wish to continue training to become teacher interns. Most of the required work could be accomplished on a part-time basis, but at least one year of formal training would be required in residence at a teacher training institution.[24]

A similar phenomenon has developed in the U.S.A. where paraprofessionals are rapidly declaring themselves as candidates for professional attainment by becoming involved in training programs that ultimately lead to certification. By seeking further education, the paraprofessionals have indicated that they are ready to acquire and apply the competencies that will enable them to do what teachers should have been doing all along: that is, to develop an atmosphere in the classroom in which effective learning can take place.

The benefits of utilizing paraprofessional assistance in the classroom have been enumerated many times in the literature.[25] Lest we hasten to support every innovation that proves effective without examining the implications for other aspects of the teacher phenomenon, however, suggests a precarious way to function. The invasion of external forces into the sacred domain of the teacher must not be viewed as a conspiracy either[26]; rather, that development must be accompanied by wise and sensitive planning - by the people whom it affects the most.

It would probably be presumptuous to suggest that every proposed school reform should obtain the blessing of teachers before it is inaugurated and under the present system this would prove impossible. The alternative would be to develop a system of school organization wherein both innovation and change could be selected, directed and inaugurated by those who are best equipped to do so. This includes even such a successful nuance as paraprofessionals in the classroom. As we shall later show, such a plan can easily be incepted and will require no major revision nor cause disruption to any component of the educational system as we know it. It is a plan that maximizes the decades of expertise and insights which are an integral part of teaching and allows for the exercise of their full professional development.

## FOOTNOTES

[1]Seymour Metzner and Jeffrey Neuman, "The Teacher Auxiliary: Aide or Maid", Urban Education, Vol. 3, No. 4, 1968, 227-233.

[2]Robert S. Patterson, et. al., Profiles of Canadian Educators, Toronto: D.C. Heath and Co., 1974, 284-285.

[3]Robert W. Richey, Planning for Teaching: An Introduction to Education, New York: McGraw-Hill, 1979, 196.

[4]Ellen Lurie, How to Change the Schools: A Parents' Action Handbook on How To Fight the System, New York: Random House, 1970.

[5]Ibid., 174-175.

[6]Robert M. Stamp, About Schools: What Every Canadian Parent Should Know, Don Mills: New Press, 1975.

[7]Ibid., 167.

[8]Stephen M. Fail, et. al., Teaching in America, Dallas: Scott, Foresman, 1979, 279.

[9]Leo W. Anglin, et. al., Teaching: What It's All About, New York: Harper and Row, 1982, 253.

[10]Douglas Myers, Ed., The Failure of Educational Reform in Canada, Toronto: McClelland and Stewart, 1973, 133.

[11]Myron Lieberman, The Future of Public Education, Chicago: Phoenix Books, 1962, 281.

[12]John I. Goodlad, et. al., A Study of Schooling, Indiana: Phi Delta Kappan, 1979 and John I. Goodlad, A Place Called School, New York: McGraw-Hill, 1983.

[13]Ronald R. Edmonds and John R. Fredericksen, Search for Effective Schools: The Identification and Analysis of City Schools that are Instruction-Effective for Poor Children, Cambridge, Mass.: Centre for Urban Studies, Harvard University, 1979.

[14]"Effective Schools Program", Schools Do Make A Difference, Calgary Board of Education, unpublished

pamphlet, 10.

[15]Ian Bazalgette Junior High School, Effective Schools Program, Program Evaluation Section, Office of the Chief Superintendent, Calgary Board of Education, June, 1984, 43.

[16]Ibid., 26.

[17]F.J. Toews and D.M. Barker, "The Baz Attack: One School's Self-Improvement Program", The ATA Magazine, Vol. 64, No. 1, November 1983, 21-23.

[18]William B. Hamilton, "The British Heritage", in Canadian Education: A History, J. Donald Wilson, et. al., Eds., Scarborough: Prentice-Hall, 1970, 35.

[19]D.W. Sylvester, Educational Documents 1800-1816, London: Newfetter Lane, Methuen and Co., 1970.

[20]Carl F. Kaestle, J. Lancaster and the Monitorial Movement, New York: Columbia Teachers' College, 1973.

[21]A. Gartner, Paraprofessionals and Their Performance: A Survey of Education, Health and Social Service Programs, New York: Praeger, 1971.

[22]J. Enns, et. al., Implications of the Employment of Auxiliary School Personnel, Ottawa: Canadian Teachers' Federation, 1974.

[23]Ibid.

[24]Bruce McLaughlin and Tagak Curley, Co-Chairmen, Learning: Tradition and Change in the Northwest Territories, Special Committee on Education, Northwest Territories Legislative Assembly, 1982, 113-114.

[25]Sr. M. Gerarda and Robert R. O'Reilly, "Acceptance of Volunteers and Teacher Professionalism", Canadian Journal of Education, Vol. 3, No. 2, 1978, 67-73.

[26]Elizabeth B. Michael, "No Conspiracy, But Let's Use Paraprofessionals Wisely", Phi Delta Kappan, Vol. 54, No. 8, 1973, 546-547.

## Chapter Four

ALTERNATIVE SCHOOLING:  SYMPTOM OF DISEASE OR CURE

The last decade has witnessed a great deal of disillusionment with public schooling to the extent that a variety of alternative schemes to the present arrangement have been inaugurated across the country. The list of pedagogical inventions includes various forms of private schooling, alternative schools within established systems, illegal schools and living room schools. In the sixties a series of free schools also dotted the Canadian educational landscape but either their format or orientation were too unbelievable for the movement to affect more than a small portion of the population. The tenure of most of these schools was relatively short-lived and only a few of them eventually gained private status or drifted into the public system as alternative schools. For the most part, reactionary forms of schooling took the form of private sector schools or alternative schools in systems which allowed them and home schooling.

Private schools in Canada are almost as old as the country itself and have always featured such characteristics as separation of the sexes, school uniforms, academic excellence as an aim, and a limiting selection process. For the most part, these schools have produced what they have claimed, namely, students with higher than average achievement and a mastery of subject matter supplementary to the provincial requirements. As the development of tax-based education gained ground in Canada, the promoters of private schools agitated for public tax support which was eventually granted on a limited basis. The debate about the legitimacy and extent of such funding is alive and well today.

The alternative school has been a more recent concept in Canada. Basically, the idea has been to offer schooling with a specific emphasis within a regularly established system, and usually this has been been motivated by religious sources, although there are exceptions. A few years ago the Calgary public system offered the Plains Indians Cultural Survival School, two Logos (Christian) Schools, two Hebrew Schools and an Alternative High School, and this pattern was not unique to the city. Today, only two of these schools remain - PICSS and the Alternative High School. Essentially, the concept was to develop schools with a special emphasis designed to meet an expressed need but with the assurance of full funding and maintenance of public standards. On a more limited level the development of second language schools originated to allow for the teaching of a variety of languages on an accredited basis via schools that operate with provincial approval, albeit only on a part-time basis.[1]

## FORMALIZING ALTERNATIVES

The arrangements for private and alternative schooling differ with each province in a number of ways, basically, perhaps because the British North America Act, which served as Canada's constitution for over a hundred years, gave educational jurisdiction to the provinces. Needless to say, this right produced a myriad of systems and structures which were either designed to meet local needs or suit the fancy of the framers of the systems.

A brief look at some of the provincial programs may prove helpful.[2]

1. British Columbia. This was the second province to recognize private schooling through a separate act of the legislature in 1977, (Quebec did so in 1968), although there is no separate school system in operation. Private schools are allowed to receive a per pupil grant for funding although the school inspector has first to recommend such on the basis that the school does not foster doctrines of racial, credal or cultural superiority and has been in operation for at least five years. A second rate of funding at a higher percentage is also available to schools which have an approved testing program, agree to school evaluations by authorities and hire only certified teachers.

2. Alberta. A wide range of options for schooling is available in Alberta with the School Act knowledging four distinct categories of schools. Category One schools follow the provincial curriculum, employ certified teachers and receive up to seventy-five percent funding based on the provincial per pupil grant. Category Two schools are private schools which cater to the handicapped or special needs students and receive similar funding. Category Three schools are special language schools which receive partial funding and operate on a limited basis provided they employ certified teachers and follow an approved curriculum. Category Four schools are supposed to use the provincial curriculum (although some do not), but they do not have to employ certified teachers nor do they receive any provincial funding.

3. Saskatchewan. Elementary private schools do not receive direct funding but they are allowed to charge fees for students from public or separate boards on a fee-for-service basis. (Secondary level schools do receive funding including partial capital grants.) These fees are recognized by the

government for grant purposes to local boards. Secondary private schools do receive funding, even partial capital grants which exceed levels awarded in Alberta. Separate high schools have recived grants since about 1965 when they were first allowed to be organized. As in Alberta, most private schools are operated by religious groups and both provinces also feature a fully tax-supported separate school system. All private schools are required to have approval of a district superintendent, although they do not necessarily have to use the provincial curriculum; alternatives can be approved.

4. Manitoba. Manitoba has a long history of educational debate originating in the Manitoba School Question of 1890 which forced the closing down of the separate school system, leaving the province with either "public" or "private" schools. Private schools receive limited direct funding since 1979, an arrangement which bypasses the benefits of a former "shared services" bill which was passed in 1965 based on an earlier Royal Commission on Education for Manitoba (1959). It is also possible for grants paid to public schools to be transfered to private schools for tuition purposes by individual school boards based on student enrolment.

5. Ontario. Elementary private schools are permitted to operate without requiring certified teachers, but at the secondary level periodic inspections are required if the school wishes to grant Ontario graduation diplomas.

6. Quebec. Granting financial aid to private schools in Quebec is virtually a necessity because the province relies on them to provide much of their secondary education. Teacher certification is mandatory to teach in either the public or the private school and there are five types of private schools in operation: vocational, schools for handicapped, self-improvement education, correspondence and general education.

7. New Brunswick. Only one kind of private school in New Brunswick receives any kind of provincial funding; there are schools for mentally handicapped schoolaged children. Other private schools must be fully independent financially.

8. Nova Scotia. A single advantage may be gained by operating a private school in Nova Scotia and that is the privilege of ordering supplies through the public system's central office. This allows private schools to obtain books and supplies at a reduced rate.

9. Prince Edward Island. Pupils attending private schools must be excused from attendance at a public school by the Minister of Education directly. No funding is available to private schools, although students are allowed the use of free textbooks while attending private schools.

10. Newfoundland. Funding is available to private schools only if they are functioning in districts not otherwise served. Teachers for these schools must be certified, provincial curriculum must be used, and the schools are

subject to periodic inspection. When these conditions are met, the school may be granted operational funding.

Private schools in Canada are subject to a fairly standard series of regulations in the various provinces in which they operate, but still have to depend on the procurement of extra fees in order to operate. In most cases they follow provincial curricula, employ certified teachers and seek to fulfill a series of educational objectives closely akin to those of the public system. Deviations include an extraordinary stress on academic excellence or religious goals. Private schools have been on the upsurge recently. In 1980-81 there were 876 such schools in Canada, 1,148 in 1983-84, and by 1986 are estimated to be in the range of 1,203, which is close to four percent of the nation's student body.[3] Financial assistance is standard practice in British Columbia, Alberta, Saskatchewan, Manitoba and Quebec, although the amounts and percentages of support varies.

Rationale

Critics of private and alternative schools sometimes find it hard to believe that anyone could be dissatisfied with a system which took years to develop, but initially, all Canadian schools could be said to be private, that is, before the provincial systems were established. In the period from 1829-1840, private and public schools in Lower Canada, for example, could be said to be indistinguishable since both received state funding, although the former were probably intended to fulfill more rigorous religious objectives. Private initiative alone was responsible for founding and operating schools and these often featured inadequate teacher preparation, few textbooks, and a whimsical curriculum. By 1787, Lord Dorchester decided to set up an Executive Council to enquire into ways and means of promoting public education.[4]

The promotion of public education in Upper Canada actually fared no better, in terms of timing, and it was 1812 before a system of state-supported schools could be inaugurated. The Loyalists had laid the ground for such a happening, some of whom were quite accustomed to having locally supported denominational schools as well as institutions of higher learning. This concern led to the formation of a school system designed to avoid the influences of republican America and foster the ideals of loyalty to the British Monarchy. There were a few examples of "plain ole" snobbery, to be sure, one being the establishment of a fine grammar school by Bishop John Strachan of the Anglican

Church at Cornwall (established in 1803), for the purpose of providing training that would get youngsters "introduced to business" in as thorough a manner as possible.[5]

More recently, private schools have come to be viewed as a kind of opposition to public schooling, and in some circles even perceived as a threat to the system. Some of the assumptions on which such schools have been developed have been construed as radical in the sense that they imply priorities which are different from the dominant objectives of public education, but it would be erroneous to suggest that their pedagogical goals are in any way antithetical to basic education.

Basically, the rationale for private/alternative education is to acknowledge that:

1. People learn in different ways, and different learning environments are essential to provide a choice for parents who want to assure maximum development on the part of their children.[6]
2. Public schools are not always able to provide the particular emphasis (religious or other values) which a constituency may prize by way of a learning environment for its children.
3. Private schools are usually smaller, thereby affording the child the attention he or she may require for the development of their learning abilities. A ponderous state system often glosses over the needs of the child because there are simply so many to service in a set period of time.
4. Smaller systems allow for greater control over such housekeeping matters as teacher selection, pupil admission, curriculum evaluation, etc.
5. Special school emphases such as academic excellence are more easily assured since the constituency for student selection is more limited.
6. Since private education usually receives less support financially than public institutions, a higher financial input will be required from supporters. This will assure a higher degree of concern and interest on the part of parents and community members. This liaison can only serve to improve the overall functioning of the school.
7. Diversity, such as private schools provide, reflects and enhances the pluralistic makeup of the nation.
8. Smaller schools, by their very nature, provide a closer working relationship between staff, pupils and parents which serves as a strong support basis for all concerned. This fact produces a school atmosphere more conducive to learning as well as to the psychological wellbeing of the child.

71

It has sometimes been suggested that a little change never hurt anyone, but even that old saw may have its limitations. Is four percent of the nation's student body enrolled in private schools too large a proportion of the population? What of the recent increase in private schooling in Canada; does this trend pose serious threats to public education as we know it?

## Analysis

The recent emergence of additional private schools in Canada is cause for concern on at least one count; this is the fact that it is not a teacher motivated development and as such is void of any professional concerns. Usually originated either by very good intentions or by a group of community dissidents with religious concerns, alternatives to public schooling are concocted on philosophical grounds - truth, values, and even reality. What is good for the teaching profession or whether relevant input may even be derived from that source is secondary. When teacher supply is ample, there is even a business angle evident, namely, to procure the best teachers available for as little money as possible. To this extent, the wellbeing of the teacher is not a consideration. Often, the starting point of such reform is also negative in tone, which may reflect on those who function in the teaching capacity. Thus, when the procurement of teachers is considered, a campaign for control may emerge which may be summarized in such declarations as, "We expect the teachers we hire to fulfill our wants regarding the education of our children." Teacher effectiveness is then viewed entirely in terms of parental concepts of high achievement on the part of the pupils, and if indeed one does fall short of the perceived goal, additional parental input may be readily forthcoming.

If it may be acknowledged that public education has shortcomings, and some of these may at least partially be rectified through alternative forms of schooling, why should such reform emanate from non-professional sources? Is there a message here for the teaching profession which is too busy, overworked or perhaps unconcerned about enhancing their field of endeavor? Philosophically, there are at least two concerns which only a professional approach can resolve: first, to provide an underlying framework for school content and process, and second, to initiate a process by which periodic evaluations can be made by which to ascertain whether formalized objectives are being attained. Andrew F. Skinner once stated that "there does not seem to be very much Canadian philosophy of education"[8], and he conjectured

72

reasons for this void as being attributable to the fact that there is altogether too much talk about educational visions, goals and issues rather than raising "why" questions, i.e., "why do we want this in the curriculum?" and "why should we teach according to a particular method?" These particular types of questions are hard to articulate and even more difficult to answer in light of the fact that a degree of philosophical sophistication is essential to properly execute the process of deduction and analysis required to ascertain if one's process is logically connected to revered goals. Reformers usually have no training and little time for an approach and prefer to react to the ills of an identified institution such as the school by hastily designing and building alternative models of operation. Small wonder that the "cure" so often resembles the disease!

Effective educational reform deserves to be engineered by those who are properly equipped for the job - the profession of teaching. What appears to be lacking, however, is for educators either to initiate relevant reforms of their own accord or to gain recognition from the community visionaries who are usually too eager to initiate their own ideas without taking the time to consult with those who might be able to steer them in a less reactionary and more worthy direction.

Unfortunately, until educators are willing to rise to the challenge of serious reform, the "war" will continue to be wrest from the control of the "generals" and mustered by the well-meaning but often ill-informed hands of the reform-mongers.

## HOME SCHOOLING

Most people are probably unaware that they have the option of not sending their children to school, and the law in all ten provinces clearly stipulates that if children are receiving satisfactory instruction in other circumstances, mandatory attendance at public institutions is not required. Provinces vary in the degree to which inspections are made regarding alternative arrangements, but, generally speaking, the system is adequate and fair. People who are aware of their freedom in this regard number about 10,000 American families and another 1,000 in Canada. Quite expectedly the trend to home schooling has raised a number of questions having to do with the enforcement of truancy laws, the ability of the family to adjust to the demands of an added function, and the general flexibility of state laws on schooling.

Reasons for extracting children from public (or private) schools are quite complex, chief of which is a disillusionment with the general impersonality of the public system and an alignment with a value scale that challenges the alleged improprieties of those entrenched in the public system.

The concept of home schooling comes at an interesting time in history, particularly in light of the fact that in many homes both parents work outside the home. In fact, the number of North American homes which fit the traditional stereotype of fathers working and mothers staying at home with the children is nine percent. How then can and will these children be educated and by whom? A partial answer to the dilemma has been a banding together of parents to accommodate their both working outside the home and educating their children at home. Parents may trade off their time away from home or devise other means of grouping so that in some homes the living room actually becomes a miniature schoolhouse.

## Origins and Rationale

One of the primary concerns of those who opt for home schooling is what they say the public school does to their children. This cause has brought together an interesting variety of viewpoints or, what John Holt calls, "strange bedfellows". It includes fundamentalistic Christians, some of whom do not have much schooling themselves, the back-to-the-landers who do not necessarily align themselves with organized religion, college educated people who grow their own food, shun meat, and have babies at home and a variety of other groups. Although they hold that public schooling has not delivered what was originally promised by the system, they differ widely in the rationale they use for the withdrawal of their children as well as on the objectives they set for their own educational enterprises. Religionists generally feel that public schools are too liberal or devoid of the moral and religious instruction they see as crucial to children's education. The other groups definitely have a specific value orientation for their objections to public schooling, although religious or theological premises are not fundamental to them. Unlike Christian proponents they are much more likely to emphasize the necessity for recognizing divergent learning styles among children.

Despite finally having achieved the goal of providing literacy to the entire nation through an institutional model, public school proponents still face the impossible task of seeking to please everyone philosophically, and, failing to do

74

so, have to enforce attendance laws. Many variations exist with regard to the approaches the American states and Canadian provinces have taken with regard to enforcement of compulsory attendance, and at times the process adopts quite despotic dimensions. In 1965 in Oelwein, Iowa, the Amish people saw their children chased into cornfields and hunted down like animals by state officers who had been rallied to enforce public education in that district. After a great deal of negative publicity emanating from a sympathetic nation who felt that the disillusionment of a small sect with schooling would not greatly interfere with the workings of nationwide education, in 1972 the Supreme Court of the USA passed a law legalizing the one-room schools operated by the Amish and the nation was again at peace. It is worthy to note that the Supreme Court decision given severe opposition by state legislators who no doubt represented the convictions of many Americans who saw even a little crack in the armour of public education as a threat to basic education. Their position could be summarized as follows: if the process of equipping the nation's young to function adequately in society is relegated to alternative arrangements on even a limited scale, the future generation would be rendered a great disservice and possibly even set literacy standards back.

The theoretical bases on which many proponents of home schooling rest their case (religious promoters excepted) lie deep in European history with appropriate North American transplants. John Dewey, who promulgated such themes as creativity, student participation in the school process and experience as the objective of schooling, built heavily on the thoughts of Jean Jacques Rousseau, eighteenth century French educator and Johann Heinrich Pestalozzi who worked in Switzerland during that time. Their work was philosophically contrasted by the efforts of John Locke who, a century earlier in England, espoused the theory of learning by rote, discipline and habit formation and that for gentlemen only. Johann Gottlieb Fichte, a disciple of Immanuel Kant, applied the theories of Rousseau and Pestalozzi to schooling in his German fatherland, arguing that the country could be revitalized through an effective school system, and Johann Herbart suggested that this could best be accomplished through a system of home schooling. Herbart lamented that national systems of education are too quickly based on political concerns with a blind disregard of individual needs. He condemned state officials who looked at the school "from on high", and questioned the notion that standardized education would lead to a revitalized nation. Herbart's platform was at least partially motivated by the polemics of Johann Fichte, who believed that Germany's rebirth was dependent on the formation of a strong system of schooling that would turn out loyal patriots. Herbart denied that politicians necessarily know anything about effective schooling and its promotion out of desperation to serve political ends would constitute an utter disregard for student needs. He suggested that an ideal German state that does not exist cannot be constructed from an ideal educational system that also does not exist.[10] His approach was to concentrate educational efforts on the individual student and to stress the accumulation of personal insight gained via individual perceptions as the important goal of education. Herbart developed a series of concepts outlining the process in "scientific" terms, i.e. the "apperceptive mass" which represented the accumulated wisdom of the mind and had a snowball effect as new knowledge was added to the vat. He suggested that attained insights never really disappear from one's knowledge store but when not "in use" slip into the realm of the subconscious from whence they can easily be withdrawn by an appropriate and relevant stimulus.

With this kind of base, Herbart was naturally in favor of schooling that would emphasize and properly appreciate the fact of individual perceptions as the basis for action, and, drawing on his own experiences in growing up and being educated with a private tutor, he advocated such a scheme for all German youngsters, impractical as that might have seemed. Like many European educators and philosophers, however, Herbart came from a well-to-do family and thus failed to appreciate the privileges of his rank. He did, however, lay the ground work for the concept of home schooling by suggesting that several families share in the expense of educating their children and thus assure both the realization of a general education and the cost of the tutor's salary.

A more rigorous analysis of educational philosophy reveals that many of the premises about learning, truth and method held to by today's proponents of home schooling are clearly parallel with the writings of North America's progressive educators: John Dewey and William Heard Kilpatrick of the USA and Hubert Newland, James L. Hughes and Loren DeWolfe of Canada. All were agreed on three premises. First, growth is dependent, not on what is done for the child but upon what the child does for himself, in other words, learning is experience. Second, developmental growth is not segmental but total. The implication of this principle is that learning cannot easily be standardized because children do not all grow at the same rate of speed nor develop in even stages. As Newland put it, "A child

76

does not shoot out an arm and then a leg. He grows all over all the time ... He grows totally all the time, in physique, intellect, emotionally, character, personality and sociality."[11] It is difficult to evaluate the rate of speed for the various components of individual education nor to determine what the totality of the learning experience would be for any group of pupils. Any attempt at standardization would have to overlook significant individual variations in any or all of these areas.

A third principle was that mental development takes place when efforts to reach a goal are evaluated. A child does not learn merely by "experiencing" something; in fact, experience is a kind of evaluation of former experience. If nothing is made of any or all of a child's experiences, they may be just ignored and rarely contribute anything to his mental development. When experiences are evaluated whether by the child or in partnership with the teacher, they attain an additional effect, or begin to affect behavior because of the extra attention they are afforded. Socrates may have said that the unexamined life is not worth living, but proponents of progressive education were not far behind when they suggested that unevaluated experiences are opportunities missed.

Proponents of home schooling are quick to point out that the numbers of pupils they handle in their "home classrooms" are small enough so that each pupil can freely share his moments of understanding with his facilitator and reap the full benefit from each personal experience. In the crowded, standardized classrooms of the public system there is far too much ground to cover that aims at socializing the child into a standard mold so that his opportunity is easily trampled. In the tradition of progressive education, they also concur that each experience is worth considering, including out of classroom activities, in the family setting or individually. When there is much ground to cover in the curriculum, of course, something has to give, and rare is the teacher who can find time to allow each of his protege to indulge his personal insights and dreams.

When Heinrich Pestalozzi, forerunner of progressive education, wrote his novel, Leonard and Gertrude in 1782, he wanted his readers to pick up on the fact that Gertrude gathered her children around her at the end of each day and encouraged them to share what had happened to them in the course of the preceding hours. She then led them in a brief but meaningful exchange or evaluation which would stamp more deeply on their minds the significant elements of their experiences. Instead, because the novel utilized the plot of a drunken husband and devoted wife, the book sold thousands of copies for the wrong reasons. Pestalozzi tried to compensate for the loss by producing a more theoretical treatise about twenty years later entitled How Gertrude Teaches Her Children but the effort was lost. No one wanted to read a series of carefully constructed, thinly veiled pedagogical principles as a story line, and since the new book had no other real message, it failed. Many home scholars today in parallel terms suggest that no one is much interested in the careful construction of educational methodologies which foster individualized instruction and the accumulation of precious personal insights because the world is too madly rushing into production models for all human enterprises. On this basis, they have withdrawn from the rat-race and afforded their children a rare opportunity in schooling.

Parents who are disillusioned with public schooling frequently conclude that such programs are built on the assumption that children are not much interested in learning, are not much good at it, and are unlikely to learn anything useful and important unless adults tell them what it is. Adults then check up on them to make sure they are learning it, using rather unimaginative means of evaluation, or rewarding and penalizing them with traditional means of reinforcement or discouragement. Critics say that educators are generally unaware of these assumptions, but function according to them because they are so deeply entrenched in the system.[12] An exception to this is the stance of the home schooling group who want more religion and values imparted to their young; they argue that the school has lost its vision of deliberate and direct socialization of the young and has gone lax in its teaching.

One of the foremost critics of public schooling in recent years is John Holt who accuses public schooling of fostering such assumptions about learning as:

1. The act of learning is passive, dull and boring.
2. Nothing is learned unless it is first taught.
3. Teaching requires specialized training and licensing.
4. Teaching is a systematic process comprising the division of materials to be mastered into subsections and presented in a sequenced fashion.
5. When children do not learn what they are taught, there is something wrong with the children.
6. All educational problems emanate from one source - the pupil.

7. An important part of the teaching-learning process is the diagnosis of problems and disorders in order that they may better function in the mainstream of prescribed content and method.[13]

Holt is undoubtedly harder on schools than he needs to be for the sake of making his point in favor of alternative education or even home schooling. It would be foolhardy to classify all educational practice as rigid and limiting as Holt does, and it is also possible that a major revamping of education as we know it (rather than a dismantling of it as Holt suggests) might rid the system of the identified ills. Without at least attempting it, we may find ourselves in the throes of the ancient warning of throwing out the baby with the bath. Certainly, if home schooling is flaunted as the alternative to the "programmed learning" machine of the twentieth century, its adoption on a wide scale (if such could even be made feasible) should be resisted until a little more light is forthcoming regarding its potential to fulfill the promises of schooling in favor of the individual.

The philosophical bases of religious groups advocating home schooling rest on grounds derived further back in the history of civilization - back to the days when it was believed that adults are totally the product of their upbringing. Little attention is paid to the progressive notions of the value of individual perceptions, creative actions which do not auger with established values or anything relativistic in terms of the quest for truth. The point is that most considerations which underly the curriculum are pretty well absolutistic in nature and if taught and adhered to in their essence will deliver a generation of moral people. Obviously schooling was once based on such notions (since all Canadian education was started by religious orders), but the pluralistic make-up of the country has decreed a more mellow tone toward philosophical positions rendered by newcomer groups, and the result has been dubbed as "secular humanism" by the fundamentalistic in-crowd. No adjustments are adequate to suit the concepts of schooling conceived by this set of home schoolers who reject even Christian private schools which were established on basically the same rationale. When the alternatives to public schooling which are inaugurated on religious grounds are considered too liberal for this segment of society one may wonder about any possible give-and-take in their stance. Obviously it would be very difficult for them to find even a neighbor who would concur with their worldly outlook on any extended scale.

## Legal Implications

A number of state, provincial and federal cases brought before the courts have supported the parents' right to educate children at home, viewing the state's right to intrude on the parents' fundamental right of privacy as limited. There are, of course, a number of conditions on which this right prevails:

1. the competency of the teachers who may be involved.
2. the teaching of subjects required by law.
3. the manner or method of teaching, so as to assure a comparable approach to that extended in the regular school system.
4. the number of hours and days devoted to schooling.
5. the availability and nature of evaluative techniques and approaches.[14]

These cases have also stipulated parents' rights and identified a series of matters into which the state may <u>not</u> enquire:

1. reasons why parents elect to bypass public schooling.
2. the nature of group experience or social environment for the child.
3. the exact nature of the curriculum if it is not officially state-approved.
4. whether or not such action creates a precedent.[15]

The concern about the child being educated in a pedagogically approved social environment has worried many educators who argue that learning is not complete when conducted in somewhat isolated situations. The primary concern is in the area of peer relations which comprise the essential ingredients for effective socialization. The areas in which student-student interaction is considered essential to the development of the child include: aspirations and goals, values and attitudes, future psychological health, social competencies, potential problem behaviors, mastery of aggressive tendencies, the development of sex role identity, perspective-taking abilities and attitudes towards schooling.[16]

The defence against these objections is that proximity of peers alone is not enough to guarantee that the above skills will be mastered. Interactions must be constructive, illustrative of social norms and fostering of such feelings as belonging, caring, support and acceptance. Home schooling proponents who favor the promulgation of a system of values which are at variance with those of dominant society, however, worry a great deal about interaction with the "right" peers. They would probably worry less about limited interaction as much as the right interaction, namely, the kind that would supplement or parallel their own beliefs.

The matter of state inspection of home schooling reveals no consistency of approach with regard to enforcement of legal requirements. No doubt many officials simply hope that the issue will dissolve as the hardships of the reality of running a school gradually diminish the enthusiasm of the supporters. If the trend continues its present rate, however, the state will have the choice of either inventing a standardized system of evaluating nonstandard means of schooling or wrestling with the challenge of formulating a flexible evaluative technique that will please both state officials as well as home schoolers. It will be a task for which the state is presently both ill-equipped and not oriented basically because uniformity is so much the norm at present.

Although home schooling is generally accepted in all Canadian provinces, seventeen American states do not make provision for it. Even when such provision exists, however, there is still the complicated procedure of providing school officials with detailed information about the exact nature of arrangements for instructing the child at home. Essentially, there are two requirements, namely having a convincing reason for doing so and ensuring an acceptable format and content, but the consequences for embarking but failing bring fines in thirty-two states and a possible jail term in twenty-one states and the District of Columbia. Evidently, the decision to educate at home is one not to be taken lightly in America.[17]

Court cases regarding compulsory school violations in the USA have revealed a number of interesting results. Generally speaking, the statutory requirement that the instructor be certified has been upheld, although exceptions have been made when it has been evident that the parent or other person in charge has at least minimal training in higher education. In People v. Levisen (404 Ill. 574, 90 NE 2nd at 214, 1950), a mother was found to be qualified because she had two years of college training and some training in education generally. In a California case where parents argued that their children were too bright to be taught in the

81

regular system, it was ruled unacceptable because the father, who was to do the instructing, did not have teaching credentials. In another case in the same state, the results indicated that "appropriate training on the part of the tutor specifically meant formal teacher training, and in People v. Turner (121 Cal App.2d 861, 263 P.2d 685, 1953), it was shown that the practice of providing a qualified tutor per se does not always warrant exemption from public school attendance.[18] The Canadian situation is significantly less rigid as was shown in Alberta when the School Act was amended a few years ago to include a Category Four type of school which did not require certification on the part of teachers nor a rigorous adherence to Alberta curriculum. The amendment was made as a result of the withdrawal of 120 children from the public school by members of the Holdeman Mennonite faith.[19] Currently, the requirements of Alberta, Manitoba, Saskatchewan, Nova Scotia and Newfoundland are the toughest and require approval of home study programs by a local school inspector. In Moose Jaw, Saskatchewan, a woman was fined $25 for keeping her daughter out of school and when she came to trial she subpoenaed thirty other families in the area who also taught their youngsters at home but none of them showed up to testify. Later, she removed her daughter from the province in search of a more receptive environment. In Ontario, a 1979 decision proved that the onus is on the school board to prove that a parent is not providing an adequate alternative to public education.[20] In the same province members of the Old Order Mennonite faith have educated their children for many years in one-room, locally controlled classrooms taught by people with only a grade eight education who make serious amendments to the provincial curriculum, i.e. lack of social studies and sciences, but the authorities have simply looked the other way. As is often the case with controversial matters, too much attention to them on the part of the state can easily ruffle feathers and backfire on those who would like to maintain the status quo at all costs. Thus the decision to go slow has been adopted by most school authorities.

## Format and Structure

After making the brave decision to educate their children at home, parents are still faced with the matter of what they will teach them and how they will proceed. Will the child or children be taught in complete isolation from any of his peers or will the banding together of several families occur. If so, who will do the teaching, all the parents alternately or only some of them?

82

To settle the matter, many parents turn to the correspondence school option and in the case of the privately operated Calvert School of Baltimore, Maryland, there are 4,500 corresponding students. Dorothy Rich, founder of the Home and School Institute in Washington, decries the stress on formal curriculum, arguing that "there is math in the bathroom and science in the sink" of any home.[21] Parents with less imagination insofar as structure is concerned often end up operating according to a school-like formula with a classroom, blackboard and library. One family in Ontario with eight children of their own found this the simplest approach and even the subject matter was divided according to the parents' area of expertise. Their children testified to a more enjoyable experience because of reduced competition with other kids normally in their classes.[22]

Home schooling carries with it to a certain extent semblances of the orientation of the nineteen-sixties when most societal institutions were under fire by the younger generation. Thus there are also instances of home schooling where virtually no curriculum is followed as parents seek to apply the philosophy that "curriculum is everywhere and learning readiness is determined by the child's perceptions and mood at any given time." One such child, Danny Williams of Thorhild, Alberta, was left to his own devices but encouraged when he showed an interest in something. Current events were a forte of his and he prepared an indepth study of many situations which attracted his fancy with appropriate encouragement by his mother.[23] Wendy Priesnitz, founder of the Canadian Alliance of Home Schoolers, suggests that families are often drawn closer together through home schooling and the arrangement also ensures a degree of self-reliance as the group strives to develop a series of workable experiences that serve to help the child reap similar pedagogical experiences to those he would gain in the traditional school setting minus the undesirable characteristics of that environment. In essence, parents who teach their children at home are not neglectful; on the contrary, they are trying to ensure a <u>better</u> education for their children.[24]

An approach not usually articulated by either side in the dispute of home schooling versus public is originated by John Holt who suggests that home schooled pupils be allowed <u>back</u> into the school setting from time to time for such events as music, sports, language etc. so as to provide the child with the opportunity to grow in the areas which cannot be accommodated at home. These would be classified as "volunteer students", even though the arrangement might initially boggle the minds of those who see formal school attendance as an all or nothing kind of situation. In essence, it is exactly that kind of inflexibility that initially gave rise to the home schooling phenomenon in the first place.

Essentially, the programs of learning for home schoolers are of two varieties - those which are designed on a rigorous basis to meet the needs of the value frame which the school is seen to have either bypassed or ignored, i.e. religious dissidents, and the more relaxed or "free" curriculum which places the onus on the child to explore or to become motivated on his own. As one proponent of the latter point of view offered, "at first we had a specific curriculum . . . but we found out that we didn't need it, so we just use it as a reference or guide." Evidently, even the children in this case needed that kind of stimulus but as the experiment got underway they began to study on their own and the role of the parent was reduced to that of facilitator or, in some instances, even that of only an interested onlooker.[25] Naturally, this view is premised on a very positive concept of the pupil as a self-starter, while that of religious promulgators of home schooling may be delineated as just the opposite. What is held in common by the two very different forces, it seems, is general disillusionment with the system, but on radically different grounds. Reform, it seems, may spring from common sources of discontent, but its extension may illustrate a myriad of philosophical assumptions.

## Analysis

Generally, when a system fails the choice for reformers is either to seek to amend or to destroy it completely. Few choose the alternative of "fleeing from the scene altogether", although this is essentially what the home schooling movement is all about. Disillusioned with what passes for formal teaching and learning, they simply pack their tents and go off to another spot in the desert. This reaction does nothing for the majority of the population caught in the institution "gone bad", if that is indeed the case, and any benefits for the child which may be discovered in the new settings are generally lost to the enterprise of education as a whole. Experiments conducted in isolation from the mainstream rarely benefit humanity, often because the orientation of the governors of reaction are too keen to share any of their new illuminations.

On a professional basis the promoters of home schooling do the teaching profession a great disservice, branding them by implication of being as unsavoury as the school system itself. This stance has several varying implications, but one obvious one is that the teaching profession matters little in the scheme of learning when teachers can so easily be replaced by well-meaning parents. This stance ignores the reality of the advance of the teaching profession over the years to the extent that we are now on the verge of injecting into the schooling process what should have been forthcoming for a long time, namely, the benefit of those years of growing as a profession.

Home schoolers also apparently see the formation and carrying out of a philosophical mandate as originating outside of the teaching realm; in other words, they do not expect relevant change to be instigated by the profession. Traditionally, it has been the case that such decisions have been made by the community via the political arena, but there is need for change. No longer can teachers merely be regarded as "a filler" in the monologue of teaching. Their expertise dictates that their opinions should shape the very nature of the enterprise in the years to come.

Home schoolers generally ignore the fact that schooling is not an uncomplicated business and it takes years to make significant shifts in terms of either philosophy or policy changes. Philosophically, there has not been a major shift in educational orientation in nearly half a century when the progressivists danced for a while on the North American educational stage and then went off into the woods. What remained of their thinking were semblances of reform that played to the tune of their convictions but which were never collaboratively assembled into a systematic whole. The open-area classroom, team-teaching, the core curriculum and the discovery method of learning were all attempts to give progressivism a chance, but the underlying philosophy of the movement was never grasped nor appreciated even in the shades in which it was articulated.

Why does educational reform have so little opportunity for survival? Two reasons may quickly be projected, one being the reluctance of the public to allow for any suggestion of change to the established system of public schooling as we know it. Only recently in major newspapers in Alberta a full-paged ad appeared sponsored by an independent group calling themselves "Save Public Education" (SPE), an organization of citizens dedicated to the preservation and improvement of public education in Alberta, bemoaned the fact that the growth of private schools is on the rise in the province, and if allowed to continue uninhibited, might actually involve 32 percent of Alberta's children by the year 2010![26] Of course, these projections are not intended to garner any semblance of rational thinking, for they do not take into account any possible factors which would auger against unlimited growth in this direction; they are obviously intended to scare people into fearing the imminent demise of the public school. For example, the fact that the Separate School System which operates in several provinces has not grown significantly over the decades since it was created, is not mentioned, and certainly the wish to grow is a vital part of the game plan of the Roman Catholic Church which governs that system.

Opponents to the possible fragmentation or even rearrangement of public schooling are quick to raise questions of elitism, segregation and tolerance when they engage in such discussion, and one often wonders what the grounds of their protectionism really are. Will the availability of a few alternatives in the system actually ruin it? Is there no implication within the democratic concept for citizen choice?

Educational reform in the future, to be believable, will need to emanate from a source more convincing than that of a few agitant citizens with a hidden agenda. Those who know best what schooling can and should accomplish will need to become the framers of the learning laboratories of the new generation - teachers. There is probably no more vital a factor in the learning experience of the child than the behavior, attitude and influence of his teachers, and no one is more aware of that fact than teachers. This necessitates not only the recognition and designing of future educational institutions to accommodate and build on that reality but that the motivation and source of planning for that endeavor originate with teacher groups. To do other is either to continue to have such reform governed by well-meaning but often ill-informed groups, many of whom have a vested interest (such as parents, who do have a legitimate interest) or to beg the question of reform altogether. That would be a tragedy.

FOOTNOTES

[1]John W. Friesen, Schools With a Purpose, Calgary: Detselig, 1983, see chapter two.

[2]T.E. Giles and A.J. Proudfoot, Educational Administration in Canada, Calgary: Detselig, 1984, 78-83.

[3]Canadian Education Association, An Overview of

86

Canadian Education, Third edition, 252 Bloor Street West, Suite 8-200, Toronto, 1984, 29.

Louis-Phillie Audet, "Attempts to Develop a School System for Lower Canada", in J. Donald Wilson, et. al. Canadian Education: A History, Scarborough: Prentice-Hall, 1970, 145-166.

J. Donald Wilson, "Education in Upper Canada: Sixty Years of Change", in Ibid, 190-213.

Giles and Proudfoot, Educational Administration in Canada, 83.

John W. Friesen, Introduction to Teaching: A Socio-Cultural Approach, Revised edition, The University of Calgary Bookstore, 1984, 55-59.

Andrew F. Skinner, "Philosophy of Education in Canada: Some Impressions and Comparative Comments" in John W. Friesen, (Ed.), Canadian Education and Ideology, Lexington, Mass.: Xerox, 1975, 13-20.

Richard A. Bumstead, "Educating Your Child at Home: The Perchemlides Case", Phi Delta Kappan, Vol. 61, October 1979, 97-100.

Val D. Reed and Frances Reed, "Home Teaching and Herbart", Educational Horizons, Vol. 58, Winter 1979-80, 75-81.

quoted in R.S. Patterson, J.W. Chalmers and John W. Friesen, Profiles of Canadian Educators, Toronto: D.C. Heath, 1974, 289-307.

John Holt, "Schools and Home Schoolers: A Fruitful Partnership", Phi Delta Kappan, Vol. 64, February 1983, 391-394.

Ibid., 392-393.

Richard A. Bumstead, "Educating Your Child at Home", 100. This list was produced by the case of Perchemlides v. Frizzle in Massachusetts, 1979.

Marion Ritter, "Read This Before You Veto Home-Education Requests", The American School Board Journal, Vol. 166, October 1979, 38-40.

[16] J. John Harris III and Richard E. Fields, "Outlaw Generation: A Legal Analysis of the Home Instruction Movement", in Educational Horizons, Vol. 61, Fall 1982, 26-31.

[17] J. John Harris III and Richard E. Fields, "Outlaw Generation", 28.

[18] Ibid., 28-29.

[19] John W. Friesen, Schools With A Purpose, chapter five.

[20] Judy Shapiro, "Home is Where the School is", Maclean's, Vol. 95, July 26, 1982, 45 and 47.

[21] J. John Harris III and Richard E. Fields, "Outlaw Generation", 28.

[22] Judy Shapiro, "Home is Where the School is", 45.

[23] Ibid., 47.

[24] Wendy Priesnitz, "Schooling at Home", Orbit, Vol. 11, January 1980, 3-5.

[25] Diane Divoky, "The New Pioneers of the Home-Schooling Movement", Phi Delta Kappan, Vol. 64, February 1983, 395-398.

[26] Calgary Herald, Monday, June 10, 1985, A14.

Chapter Five

DELIVERING ON THE DOLLAR:   EDUCATION AS A COMMODITY

It would be erroneous for anyone to suggest that attempts have not been made to revamp the school system as we know it, although the envisaged schemes have never been fully developed.  The kinds of efforts discussed in this chapter have primarily been originated in the United States but with little success; similar proposals have also been voiced in parts of Canada.[1]  Essentially these reforms are structural in essence with corollary implications or designs for the teaching role, parental choice or financial base.  The three most popular kinds of reforms have to do with educational vouchers, educational tax credits and performance contracting.

## EDUCATIONAL VOUCHERS

The quest to build the factor of choice into schooling has been growing in recent decades and one of the proposed ways of accomplishing this has been through a voucher system.  In this arrangement, parents would be given access to direct money grants which they could trade for the education of their children at the school of their choice.  An underlying assumption was that parents would feel more committed to a school if they had a greater voice in its selection, and teachers would be more responsible because of the added pressure to "compete in the market" for students.  In addition, the arrangement would guarantee that school programs would more nearly reflect the wishes of the constituency in terms of curriculum wants or school environments.  Individual needs of students would also be met to a greater degree as flexibility and a catering to constituent demands would be standard elements in the arrangement.

The first real publicized attempt to introduce a voucher system occurred in 1955 when Milton Friedman, an economist, decided that government monopoly in education was a threat to the system itself.[2]  His proposal received widespread acceptance and proponents for the plan sprang up quickly in all sectors of American society.[3]

The Voucher Plan

Friedman's original proposal was a relatively unregulated concept but it was aimed at limiting government involvement in the school enterprise.  He suggested that individual schools should be able to set their own admission standards so long as they did not offend the freedom of any American children. They should not be allowed to discriminate in student selection, although tuition costs for participating schools could vary; schools, in fact, could make extra charges to parents who wanted a "better" education for their children but the assurance had to be realized that the country's population would have equal access to basic education anywhere in the nation.

By the late 1960's the voucher idea had been picked up in various parts of America, many of them applauding the concept of competition among schools. Theodore Sizer, the dean of the Harvard Graduate School of Education, suggested that vouchers only be given to poor children with a sliding scale so that government subsidy would decrease as family incomes rose. Another Harvard academic, Christopher Jencks, argued for careful government regulation and claimed that no parent should be allowed to supplement the government voucher with his own private resources. He also suggested that children from poor families receive a special compensatory voucher that would make their presence more acceptable to schools in a free market.[4] The arrangement was viewed by Jencks as an opportunity to make resources available to schools for solving some of the problems that children generally bring to school.

Many variations of the voucher plan emerged in the USA over the next decade of which the following characteristics were typical: (i) schools could charge what they wanted so long as they provided scholarships for the poor, the condition being that the amount would be determined by an agency and based on family income; (ii) tuition could not be more than the voucher amount and financial assistance could be lobbied for by each school; and (iii) schools would be rewarded for student achievement, and penalized for failure to bring about achievement; achievement levels could be determined by scores on standardized tests. From looking at these models one can see the different goals implicit in them. Some are directed at applying market theory to schooling in order to encourage competition, while others augur for a regulated system that would expand freedom of choice. The latter see the need for enhancing diversity in the school so that individual needs may be maximized.

A survey of the various voucher models prepared by David G. Young of the University of Alberta is helpful in delineating the basic concept:[5]

1. The Friedman - Unregulated Market Model.

Households would be issued vouchers with the same redeemable value for each child at the institution of the parent's choice. All schools could charge tuition to the amount of the voucher which would be legislated initially at a level equal to the existing cost of educating a child in any given district.

2. The Sizer-Whitten - Unregulated Compensatory Model. Here the value of the voucher would be higher for poor children. Essentially, schools could charge whatever tuition they wanted, but families with incomes above the national average would receive no subsidy. At a given point the value of the voucher would be zero.

3. The Jencks Private Membership Model. Again, schools could charge as much tuition as they liked provided they gave scholarships to children from lower income families. A Central Voucher Agency would establish a formula by which to show how much people at each income would be charged.

4. The Coons-Sugarman Effort Voucher Model. This model established several different possible levels per pupil expenditure and allowed the school to set its own level. Parents who chose higher levels of tuition type schools would have to come up with the extra cash. Poor families could do the same and draw on their voucher potential to cover the cost of tuition.

5. The Egalitarian Model. Here the value of the voucher would be the same for each child land no school would be allowed to charge extra tuition. Schools, instead, would be able to solicit money for special programs from government and private sources or encourage fund raising via community or support organizations.

6. The Achievement Model. The value of the voucher would be based on progress made by the child during the year. Schools would be rewarded if their pupils exceeded predicted scholastic levels or penalized if the reverse occurred. Schools could contract achievement levels where monies were proportional to gains on standardized tests.

7. The Jencks - Regulated Model. Here schools could not charge tuition beyond the value of the voucher, but they could earn funds by accepting children from poor families or educationally disadvantaged children. A variation of this approach allowed privately managed voucher schools to charge affluent families according to their ability to pay.

Of the above models, only the Jencks regulated compensatory model was close to being tested and it, along with the Coons-Sugarman model (known also as the California Family Choice Program) will be described here. The unofficial name of the Jencks project is "The Alum Rock Experiment".

91

The Centre for the Study of Public Policy at Cambridge, Massachusetts, initially set about testing the voucher system by establishing several demonstration programs in heterogeneous communities. Primarily concerned with under privileged children, they recommended that initial grants be given to selected communities and the demonstrations themselves were to last from five to eight years. In September, 1972 the Community of Alum Rock, California decided to implement the plan on a large scale, the only one of several American communities to really do so. Because of the appreciation for innovation the community was allowed to make significant changes to the basic model, first of all by involving only six of its sixteen schools, all of them public.

The Alum Rock experiment began by developing a controlling centre known as the Educational Voucher Agency that would ensure that a school's eligibility by requiring a certain curriculum and assuring the avoidance of discrimination in its operation. Every aspect of the participating school's program was investigated, including transportation and staffing. Specifically, the following policies were then adopted: (i) No school would charge tuition beyond that allowed by the voucher; (ii) Compensatory vouchers were given to poor children to provide them with incentives for attending schools; (iii) If a school had more applicants than space, its personnel must fill out at least half of the positions available by a random means; and (iv) Schools were responsible for providing information to parents.

The results of the Alum Rock experiment were intriguing to say the least. Influenced to a large extent by the nature of the project rules and the school population itself, the participants included students from several specific ethnocultural groups - fifty-five percent Hispanics, ten percent Blacks, and thirty-five percent other such groups. Choice was given to parents insofar as enrollment of their children was concerned, and the autonomy of the school with regard to operation was assured. A questionnaire involving 600 participants was the basic tool utilized to determine the success of the enterprise, and a control group was established for comparisons. It was soon discovered that teachers found the experience to be very enjoyable and professionally intriguing. Enrollments stabilized after the first two years and the project's teachers found themselves able to cope with the business of educating without much further such adjustment. Essentially, results of the research were inconclusive, although it was found that amount of education influenced the way parents perceived the project.

Those with less formal education were less likely to pay attention to printed materials made available by the experiment's promoters, and unlike their better educated peers they also made choices for their children for other than educational reasons.

Teacher enthusiasm for the voucher system emanated from the fact that they felt they had greater control over curriculum, budget and staffing decisions, although this varied from one school to another. Teachers frequently identified very strongly with their particular school and were reluctant to transfer if the need arose. Although only a half dozen schools were involved, these were further subdivided into twenty-two "mini schools". Specifically, teachers cooperated to the extent that conditions in their mini-system were not threatened. One complaint was that the competitive nature of the experiment added to the amount of problems they faced in the regular system instead of solving them. Thus the dilemma arose that if problems were even partially seen to be solved the enrollment of the school would increase and these problems would be enhanced.

Enrollment figures in the schools involved in the project fluctuated. After an initial increase of up to sixty percent in one mini-school, a ten percent figure of change appeared to normalize. As choices became stabilized, variations in enrollment between years two and three became more moderate. Insofar as choice was concerned, parents appeared to take advantage of their options to a marked degree in the initial stages of the plan and later either wearied of it, saw no real differences in approaches or simply became concerned with other matters.

Critics of the Alum Rock plan range widely in their opinions, some claiming that the operators did not go far enough in the quest to encourage choice or, for that matter, to make genuine options available. Apparently, some schools took action to reduce their vulnerability by building cash revenues and placing limits on acceptance of students and enrolments. The fact that public schools only were included was another concern, thus limiting the testing in an important facet. Still, the founders of the idea reiterated a series of advantages which were hard to deny. These included smaller classes, more attention to the needs of the slow learner and the high achiever, parental choice in education, and the inclusion of multi-age groups in the student body.[6]

On the negative side were several notable critics like John Gardner and R. Freeman Butts, with the latter bemoaning the idea that the voucher system would destroy the public form of schooling, an institution that was envisaged by the founders of the notion as a means of preparing the young for the role of self-governing citizens rather than as subjects. Butts warned against the "danger" of the experiment on historical grounds - it would destroy Thomas Jefferson's dreams for a participatory democracy and feed the appetite of privatism.[7] These criticisms got underway even before the experiment was completed or the results of testing were in. In a sense, there was fear of any kind of revamping of America's education in the minds of many Americans.

A second test of the voucher concept was started in California in 1979 called "California's Family Choice Initiative". It was designed by John Coons and Stephen Sugarman of the University of California at Berkeley who conceived the idea of a series of independent schools that would be created by a vote of existing school boards. The necessity of such a vote would come about via a petition with enough signatures from interested parents within a particular school district. Incentives for developing such schools would be fostered by a deregulation of existing rules to provide additional flexibility, and the schools could be developed by either parental groups or other interest groups. Schools could establish their own kind of administration patterns but they would not be allowed to charge more tuition than the voucher amounts. The school could determine its maximum size and if it had more applicants than could be accommodated a lottery system would have to be inaugurated. Children could be expelled only for extraordinary reasons.[8]

Standard features of the California Family Choice program included teacher bargaining, tax originated financial base, and arrangements for special student needs. There was also a system of teacher awards for those who filled the office well, part of the basic philosophy to guarantee the best education for all. What was unique about this idea was to create real variation in school program and orientation, but the traditional notion of operating schools via a publicly elected board of trustees remained. Although the system was never inaugurated because of a failure to garner the needed number of votes (1980), proponents were anxious to gear up for a second try at a later date.[9]

Evaluating the Voucher Concept

It is difficult to formulate a device to evaluate the various voucher plans because each of them is designed on a slightly different basis, and only one of them was ever really tried. One of these factors in assessing any of the proposals is the role of government; some plans propose a limited role in terms of distribution of vouchers only while others would forsee some involvement in terms of a delivery as well. A still further involvement might pertain to the assurance of non-discriminatory practices or to manage available school space to assure maximum usage among the participating schools in a given district.

Philosophically, the voucher concept promulgates many revered ideas among avant garde educators - economic equality, healthy competition, commitment, shared values and a broader scale for educational advancement. Accountability would be more specifically directed at parents, thereby assuring a more explicit meaning to the notion of democratic rights, and a wider range of schools from which to choose would also relieve pressures on sectarian and private schools.

On the negative side of the ledger is the protest that schools are not particularly good institutions to be charged with the mandate of equalizing social opportunities and the plan would, in fact, have the potential to create a system of "private" schools supported by public funds. The claim to avoid discriminatory practices is another concern of voucher critics who suggest that elitism could result from the use of such criteria as income, academic ability or religion if utilized as a basis for admission. The exact nature of the process can hardly be guaranteed, and that would make it highly susceptible to personal ingenuities in giving the appearance of equality. Finally, the exclusion of religious schools from the voucher system, some argue, would leave the public system virtually unchallenged anyway.

Philosophically, the question needs to be raised as to the feasibility of converting a "soft-ware" enterprise like schooling into a business model. What kind of educational reforms can be expected from subjecting schooling to a model based on profit and loss statements? Are the concerns of the two systems on the same wave length? Furthermore, what are the assurances that both the initial concept and continual monitoring of the process will have essential pedagogical input from trained educators? If the system is run by traditional functionaries and based on established notions of what schooling can or should do, will the result really be any different?

Frequently, private schools are held up to be an example of the potential success of a voucher system with the corollary argument that these schools "play to an open market" and fare quite well at it. What is different, however, is the fact that private schools cater to a select market (usually from the religious community), and what they offer is not envisaged to be in the same category as the basic education offered by the public system. Private schools usually have to charge tuition rates that are not always affordable by lower income groups (unless by very dedicated people), and they feature a reduced student-teacher ratio. Some of these schools also utilize an entrance test that assures them of a select student body; this the voucher schools would not be allowed to do.

The economic base on which the voucher debate has raged has some philosophical ground, but little of it has been directed toward the improvement of or rights of the teaching profession. John Coons pleads for an equitable system of schooling that will once and for all eliminate the class segregation in schooling as we know it[10] and Sugarman stresses the need to restore choice into the enterprise. He suggests that "there is no consensus over what are the proper goals and means of education"[11] so why not let people choose the kind of education they want for their children (within limits, of course). Paul Goodman completes the list by expressing some sympathy for the concept of the voucher school but complains about the lack of attention afforded "essential knowledge and universal truths" in education today.[12]

It will remain for another time and another place to recommend educational reform that will acknowledge the proper place of the true educator - the teacher.

## TUITION TAX CREDITS

Unlike the Canadian system where individual provinces have a greater say in educational matters, the United States has a much more standardized delivery system of schooling and more restrictive rules by which to function. This is particularly true with regard to school funding which traditionally applied only to public schools. Private schools, religious or otherwise, were on their own. On April 15, 1982, something happened that changed all that, when

96

President Ronald Reagan addressed the annual meeting of the National Catholic Educational Association and announced that he would install a means whereby parents who opted for private schools for their children would be able to deduct a portion of that tuition charge from their income tax.[13] Immediately another classic debate broke out with critics lining both sides of the ring.

Reagan's rationale for making this proposal included the observation that America is (typically) the greatest and freest nation in the world. Yet, in a free land, people were not being given the right to education of their choice without penalty. Reagan professed to change all that at least in a limited fashion but limited only because he was restricted from applying the scheme to the college level because of the fiscal restraints operant in the USA in 1982. Reagan reiterated many themes common to American education in his address including reference to the Pledge of Allegiance, but insisting that he was on the side of improving education by encouraging alternatives, not tearing it down. He suggested that since knowledge is intricately tied up with freedom, alternatives in American education would only serve the best interests of the cause if different avenues of the pursuit were encouraged. He also implied that the nation's poor would benefit from the proposal because they would be helped to afford to educate their children in some of the nation's finest schools if they chose to do so. In the words of the Most Reverend James P. Lyke of Cleveland whom the President quoted, "You [the poor] may now educate your children in the school of your choice as guaranteed by the Constitution, and you will be able to do so, even though you may be poor, whether you live in the city of the suburbs or the rural areas of this country."[14]

The movement for support of tuition tax credits actually began in the USA in the nineteen sixties when private school enrollments declined drastically. Supporters rallied to ask the government to sustain such schools as an important alternative to public education but only managed to preserve the tax-exempt status of the schools. By the 1970's enrollments in private schools climbed, partially as a result of mandatory segregation, and parents increased their complaints about having to pay taxes for a public system which they did not utilize. Under the Carter Administration what was called the Packwood-Moynihan Tuition Tax Credit Bill was prepared which was to allow private school supporting parents a maximum of 50% of their tuition costs up to a maximum of $500.

The Bill was defeated on the basis that it would cost the country too much in lost taxes. Reagan's proposal captured the essence of the positive nature of Packwood-Moynihan proposal and may have been encouraged because of the positive nature of the Coleman Report on private schools. Reagan proposed an initial amount of $100 in tax credits per elementary and secondary student in 1983, $300 in 1984 and $500 from then on.

## Highlights of the Debate

Central to any debate on education in America is the Constitutional matter of the separation of church and state. The vast majority of the literature on the subject is in favor of the proposal to allow tax credits, and most defenders justify their stand constitutionally on the basis that these credits can be used only by the individual, not by institutions. This apparently circumvents the possibility of constitutional violation, but does not still the voices of those who favor public education at all costs. This group claims that if private or parochial education is assisted in this manner, it will ultimately undermine public education. If the ground for ensuing this path is the assumption that public education has failed in some way, additional money should be given to public schools so they may improve in the areas in which they have been found wanting.

Proponents of tuition tax credits argue that private schools have a legal and democratic right to exist because of the justice implied in the American pluralist principle, and maintain that poor families would benefit most from such a scheme. In a sense they are correct in that the majority of parents with their children in private schools in the USA earn $25,000 a year or less.[15] When sending their children to private schools they bear not only the cost of their children's education but pay taxes to support the local public school as well. That, the proponents contended, can hardly be considered an expression of American fair play.

Perhaps the most common complaint about tuition tax credits is that they foster the demise of the public system. Hawkins argues that the public system is presently overburdened with assignments, having to be "all things to all people" and is thus unable to deliver. Besides having to provide students with a sound education, schools have been asked to increase custodial functions, to become active in civil rights and assure services to the handicapped. These are certainly laudable goals, but many of them are simply beyond the capability of the institution because they require a specialization which is impossible for a generalist institution to deliver. Combined with this is a burgeoning movement in the USA for the schools to return to "the basics".[16] On the positive side, tuition tax credits may actually serve as a motivator for public school supporters to seek reform; if the movement is properly directed it will solicit advice from the American public and possibly assure them the kind of education they believe their children require. This, instead of being contrary to the American way, will assure it. It will almost certainly provide credibility to the axiom that citizens through reflection and choice can create good governments rather than relying on their political constituents who by[17] accident or force may decide what is best for the people.

The accusation that public schooling in America is falling short of expected achievement levels has some support in the S.A.T. College Board Examinations and Short Common Tests which show a steadily declining student performance over the years. In 1977, a special panel established by the College Board, set out to determine the cause for the decline and reported a variety of reasons in their report including school[18] centralization and lower teaching standards. If the results of the Coleman Report may be juxtaposed to this situation and the case for private schools made more strongly, it might appear to be ample justification to supply some credit (including tax) to a successful way of schooling. If the dollar sign is as significant as it has been in North American educational planning, this comparison might actually constitute an argument for even great tax support than President Reagan offered.

Robert Baldwin has extended the case for tax credits on the basis that diversity in schooling can bring harmony to the American community and foster more, better and cheaper schools. He argues that the nation has grown increasingly diverse in thought and created now value systems and if these differences were accommodated in the school system it would provide a higher degree of happiness to the citizenry and contribute to the quality of life. Those who oppose diversification frequently express fear that the public system will eventually be dismantled via such a plan, but Baldwin's figures project that a maximum of twenty-five percent of any given constituency would opt for any change in education[19] even if given the opportunity. By parallel, if the public schools are so good, why has there been a constant clamour on the part of a significant percentage of the population for change in recent decades. Alternatives may be the best insurance and incentive for improvement.

A phenomenon frequently referred to by proponents of tuition tax credits pertains to the way in which the arrangement would help lower income groups to achieve some measure of acknowledgement of their preferences in tax reform. The proposal would actually put a little more money into the pockets of contributing families, perhaps little more than a token of appreciation.

Insofar as elitism and inequality are concerned supporters argue that the current system of public schooling has a far worse record in this area than do private schools. Thus the latter should be encouraged to function. Since private schools do not segregate now it will be even less justifiable to accuse them of it once more parents are able to truly choose their schools. The opportunity for underprivileged classes to experience better education may also be enhanced by the fact that parents will be able to promote racial harmony on a voluntary basis rather than being forced to do so. This result will be achieved through higher quality of education in cities which will follow from market competition encouraged through tuition tax credits. With quality education thus available in cities, middle class families will have reduced incentives to move to the suburbs as a way of ensuring a good education for their children. As Sowell indicates, the swell of flights to suburbia has increased to include numbers from minority group backgrounds as well as predominantly white middle class families.[20]

A breakdown of figures pertaining to current enrollments in private schools suggests that the urban poor might find advantage in the tuition tax credit system if the example given by Sister Renee Oliver is any indication. According to a survey made by the Catholic League for Religious and Civil Rights of fifty-four inner city private schools, seventy percent of the enrollment were of minority background. These schools were located in New York, Los Angeles, New Orleans, Chicago, Milwaukee and Washington, D.C. The results indicate that not only are the poor looking to private schools to provide their children with the academic and moral education they will need in adult life, but also that the tuition tax credit bill will help the parents of those children financially.[21] The exact nature of this saving breaks down thusly. If current tuition costs in American private schools were raised even $15.00 per month, only thirty-six percent of the families included in the survey said they could afford to continue sending their children to private schools. Twenty-eight percent said they would definitely have to withdraw their children from these schools.[22] It would appear, then, that even such small amounts of savings as those projected in the Reagan proposal would have a significant impact on a great number of parents of marginal incomes. Given these terms, the proposal should carry a lot of weight on the American educational scene.

As the arguments swing back and forth in the tuition tax credit war, it is useful to compare some statistical renderings from the other side of the debate. Catterall and Levin, for example, contend that minority group enrollment in private schools is actually low. Quoting from national census figures in the USA, they suggest that Black children account for fourteen percent of all high school enrollments but only six percent of private school enrollments. The discrepancy is smaller for Hispanic children.[23] When one considers the percentage of all American children enrolled in private schools, however, the picture is less severe than Catterall and Levin imply. Their argument is based on "relatively low numbers of children" rather than the number of enrollees in comparison of population proportion. The same line of reasoning is evident with respect to average wage earnings of private school supporters. These authors argue that sixty percent of private high school families earn more than $20,000 per year, but as we have earlier pointed out according to another source, the majority of parents supporting private schools earn $25,000 a year or less.[24] Both sources were published in 1982 and appear to suggest a bit of discrepancy or line of interpretation.

Analysis

Essentially, the groundswell in favor of tuition tax credits rests on the same philosophical laurels as the voucher proposals. The central task is to meet social needs, e.g. special needs of lower income groups and to promote a more equitable system of education. Related advantages include a reduction of financial pressures on private schools through increased parental commitment and enthusiasm. Research on private education has shown this to be the case and that fact has been interpreted to suggest that smaller targets of commitment which private schools represent are objects of intensified dedication.[25]

Proponents of both the voucher system and tuition tax credits suggest that the public system is out of touch with the needs of society. The cure for this apparent dilemma, however, is not really targeted on one particular sector of the enterprise for who should be consulted, namely, the teaching profession. A few proponents contend that teachers would have more power in shaping school curriculum in an enhanced "private school system" such as the tuition tax credit arrangement implies, and the same rights as they are currently in possession of would be assured in the revised plan. Another advantage would be increased job opportunities as new schools would be created or a reshuffling might occur in current systems as their objectives are enhanced or revamped. Generally speaking, the development would also provide the same professional benefits for teachers in private schools as their public counterparts now enjoy.

Perhaps the greatest omission in the tuition tax credit concept is that even if incepted it would perpetuate the current bureaucratic structure. Administratively, there would be few changes except that the layering of officialdom might be rearranged. The voice of the teaching profession would not be altered in any significant fashion except that if the private school model is adhered to more closely in the proposed system, teachers might find themselves working in a closer liaison with parent groups and trustees than they currently experience in the public system. The possibility of salvaging such a development to some extent could possibly be brought about if sufficient teacher representation could be assured on the regulatory body responsible for operating the new system, but this is not implied in any of the related literature.

To reduce parental input or advice in the school function is never an advisable route in school reform, and the tuition tax credit vision ensures this by way of constantly stressing enhanced parental choice. To increase, revise or provide alternative means of bureaucracy without properly acknowledging the insights of the teaching profession is sheer pedagogical folly. While it would probably be difficult to eliminate the market factor in public institutional operations, it might still be beneficial to scrutinize how best to endorse such a model in terms of any proposed administrative patterns, philosophy, content and objectives. Undoubtedly, the best group to consult with in that regard (and perhaps assign greater authority) is the education profession, the "silent" majority in the schooling enterprise.

## PERFORMANCE CONTRACTING

The decade of the seventies witnessed a new phenomenon on the educational scene as critics of the schooling process cried out for greater accountability to ensure productivity. Dissatisfied with the performance of schooling generally, a trend soon began to award some of the school's functions to private industries which promised greater guarantees than educators in the public education system. Essentially, performance contracting means just that - an agreement made between an educational authority and a private corporation in which the latter agrees to supervise and/or conduct particularized learning activities which will result in specified levels of attainment as assured by mutually agreed upon criteria, and in which the former pays the corporation fixed amounts for certain performance levels per pupil within specified times.[26]

The rationale for electing to initiate performance contracting was derived from several assumptions, one of them being the notion that the education system is supported by the community and should be accountable to the community. By contracting educational activities to a private source, that accountability would be much more evident than what the school could or had delivered since industry would be trying harder to accomplish announced goals. Another concern had to do with the complaint that schools are too oriented toward the average student and the low achiever is often neglected. By assigning teaching tasks specifically related to the individual student needs, pressure to perform would increase on the part of the private entrepreneur and learning would be enhanced.[27] Performance contracting proponents also argued that a different environment than "normal" was necessary to motivate the slower learner to achieve; they contended that the higher achiever learns through pressure from his peers, but the slow learner is not thusly motivated. Therefore, to take the slow learner away from the school environment would serve to produce the kind of atmosphere in which he is given the desire to learn. That atmosphere would be based on gaining material rewards, a concept which is alien to the regular form of schooling but which would be allowable under extenuating circumstances such as performance contracting could deliver.[28] Experiments of an extraordinary nature were never allowed in the schools, it was argued, part of the problem being that administrators were usually too busy to pay much attention to new possibilities or procedures. Consequently, slow learners and other groups of students were often neglected because of the rush to get on with the assigned process. As an outsider, the performance contractor could devise his own kind of environment in which even radical ways of teaching could be introduced. There were some educators who quickly argued against the incentives plan on the basis that it could become part of the socialization process and thus confuse the student into believing that life functions only according to rewards and penalties for performance.

Initially, the concept of performance contracting was based on the idea that only bona fide educators would be employed by contracted firms in order to assure a proper quality of delivery. No contract was to be negotiated that would tend to compromise the school system's integrity or its responsibilities to children. Care was also taken to avoid signing contracts just because they had been made to look attractive by some clever sales gimmick, and the motivation of the firm employed was checked out to ensure that the program would not simply deteriorate into a propaganda campaign or the pursuit of the self-interest of the company. Another caveat included an appraisal of the company's contract with regard to the inclusion of professional attitudes, ideas and motivations since the field was full of prospective agents almost as soon as the movement got underway. The assumption which many proponents from within the educational world promulgated on was that most industries were probably honest and upright but extra precautions needed to be taken because the nation's children were involved in the process. That fact remained at the bottom of the controversy that ensued over the next decade.

The performance contract movement rested heavily on the notion of accountability, suggesting that playing to that piper would also augur well for the teaching profession. Lessinger suggested a series of ways in which this might happen:

1. The focus of teaching would shift from lecturing and "telling" to one of product, and teachers would be relieved of their babysitting functions to spend more time in marshalling resources, prescribing alternatives and providing feedback.
2. Patrons of schools would come to understand the important difference between teaching and learning, and teachers will thus be able to use a much wider variety of non-school resources.
3. The criteria for education would change from one of input to achievement. That which "works" would be the criterion of the success of the process.
4. Teacher training would be changed to rely on competence in achieving student learning as a prerequisite to certification.
5. Salary levels would move to impressive levels once teachers were able to demonstrate their true abilities.
6. The performance contract would become a stable element in the schools as teachers used it to bring new and better ways of teaching into the classroom on a carefully supervised basis.[29]

104

The American Federation of Teachers issued a statement of opposition to performance contracting as it got underway on the basis of several different concerns. They announced that they would oppose any performance contracting plan which would:

1. take the determination of educational policy out of the hands of the public and place it in the hands of private industrial entrepreneurs;
2. threaten to establish a monopoly of education by big business;
3. threaten to dehumanize the learning process;
4. sow discord among teachers through a structured incentive program;
5. promote "teaching to a standardized test";
6. subvert the collective bargaining process and reduce teacher input; and
7. be predicated on the assumption that educational achievement can be improved in the vacuum of a machine-oriented classroom, without changing the wider environment of the poverty-stricken child.[30]

Teachers were not alone in their objections to the practice of making educational contracts with private business, and many critics questioned the wisdom of trying to run schools like businesses. They argued that the differences between the two institutions were too great to merge simply by means of a contract (which was a business concept anyway). Thomas Shannon accumulated a series of eight reasons why schools aren't businesses:

1. Private business has the single goal of making a profit, whereas public education has multiple objectives and its successes are measured by an entirely different (social and psychological) process.
2. Business is headed by directors and managers with considerable homogeneity of purpose, while public education is governed by political governing boards who are directly responsible to the electorate.
3. Business is an employer, and public education is both an employer and a governmental entity.
4. Private business works with labor unions which are oriented toward the private sector while public education deals with unions that are quasi-political entities.
5. Private business managers enjoy a great deal of discretion in managing an enterprise; conversely, public educators have a detailed set of constraints

to adhere to.
6.  Business has a sharply defined top leadership group that enjoys an abundance of freedom in dealing with its managers, while educational managers are a much more amorphous group who possess more job security than their counterparts in private industry.
7.  In business, power and influence remain in the business itself, but in public education external constituencies are capable of exerting much influence on educational governance.
8.  If defamed in public, business managers have a ready resort to redress in the courts, but public educators are prime targets for community redress and they have virtually no protection against slander and libel.[31]

Despite the criticisms levelled at the plan, performance contracting was formally installed in several different American school systems for experimentation. In February 1972, the US Office of Economic Opportunity (OEO) completed a $7.2 million study of performance contracting it conducted independently with eighteen urban and rural school systems and six contractors during the 1970-71 school year. Although the report was not positive, it would be unfair to pass condemnation on the experiment without examining its procedures and claims.

The Performance Contracting Plan

For humanists, the procedure for performance contracting may actually be considered quite crass. Contracts call for a certain amount of learning for a certain amount of dollars. Period. In one contract in Grand Rapids, Michigan, the school board agreed to pay the contractor $75.00 for each student who gained a year of reading achievement, $112.50 for any student who gained one and a half years and $127.50 for any student who gained two full years, and still more for greater gains. What were called "interim performance objectives" were also invented (worth $37.50 each) and which were payable at intervals during the period of the experimentation. This arrangement was one of eighteen such contracts negotiated by the US Office of Economic Opportunity.[32]

Defenders of the plan, like business leaders Charles Blaschke and Reed Martin, argued that the purely incentive process is a bit overdone, and although they concede that it might be difficult to incept, it is possible to foster

106

educational reform with quite humane elements built into it. Blaschke, in fact, insisted that a good performance contract would include:

1. a low risk/low cost means of experimentation;
2. an educationally effective, politically palatable means for racial integration;
3. a feasible means to facilitate community and parent control and involvement;
4. a means to rationalize the collective bargaining process;
5. a means to humanize the classroom for both teacher and student; and
6. a means to increase instructional efficiency in such areas as math and reading.[33]

Blaschke also argued that positive teacher characteristics like smiling at students can stimulate academic growth, and even feigned attempts to practice such, on the part of the teacher, can eventually become viable ways of behaving.[34] Blaschke does not view performance contracting as the introduction of either a foreign philosophy or partner into the educational process, contending that it is a new way to rearrange the relationships of all legitimate participants in the educational process, new and old.[35]

Although both math and reading were prime targets for performance contract assignments, there were also schools where every subject became part of the contract arrangement. As an example of the kind of contracts that were given out, during the summer of 1970 the Reading Foundation of Chicago contracted with a school near Los Angeles (Compton Unified School District) for $110,000 to operate a speed reading program for that school year. All regular seventh graders were scheduled into the program for a total of nine weeks and the major performance objective was stated as follows: "Seventy-five percent of the students in the program will increase their reading speed five times over their beginning level with ten percent more comprehension after twenty-four hours of instruction and twenty-two hours of outside reading."[36] The program also included the following components: lectures focusing on the willingness and ability to read faster, practice speed tests, use of pacers, tachistoscope exercises, and a reading assignment of fifty-eight books. While the Reading Foundation claimed that the students had made significant gains in both speed and comprehension, the results were disputed by educational critics who pointed out that they had made use of diagnostic tests for evaluative purposes and these should not have been used. Another criticism was the manner in which progress was measured. Students were given periodic tests to determine speed and comprehension and the scores they received were rendered as the number of words read in a given time multiplied by the percentage of comprehension attained. Thus a student could "read" at a very fast rate, achieve a very low comprehension score and still appear to have made progress from his previous pace. Also, many students noticed that the answers to their comprehension test were only one page removed from the test itself which made easy access to the answers and may have influenced the results dramatically.[37] In another situation, it was found that twenty-five percent of a particular group of students showed a year's gain in reading due to a simple test error.

Aside from digging away at the details of the above experiments there are some underlying assumptions to be wrestled with in examining the claims of the performance contracting phenomenon. Primarily, the movement grew out of the "usual" concern that the schools were not doing their job. A desire to fix a measure of accountability on teachers developed, coupled with industries' boast that "we can do it better." The latter assertion was probably backed by a belief that productivity and accountability are key phrases in the business world and they would easily be adapted to the educational realm as well. Essentially, some contenders insisted, it is a matter of management, and its proper execution depends on the process of meaningful negotiation and the built-in assurance of accountability. The stress on material values, of course, cannot be left out of any evaluation because the basic procedures of the contracts made with students, for example, were just that. In some cases, students who achieved a desired level in reading received a transistor radio. Lesser rewards included Green Stamps or ten minutes of listening to rock music.[38] To suggest that the program was not based on a very specific set of values would be to beg the question.

Albert Yee very impressively makes the point that while the decision-makers of a decade or two ago expressed great optimism and even self-assured arrogance in their belief that rational prescriptions for the improvement of society could be designed and implemented - especially to erradicate poverty, improve the economy and devise complex, fail-safe defense mechanisms - they were wrong. Flow charts do not easily reveal the workings of the affective creature, man.[39]

Evaluating Performance Contracting

One of the most discussed experiments in performance contracting was launched in the early fall of 1970 in Texarcana, border town of the two states for which it was named. Eighteen school districts were involved with six firms being awarded contracts for some aspect of the teaching-learning situation. Every major geographical area and every major racial and ethnic minority were included - Puerto Rican, Mexican-American, Black, Eskimo, Indian, etc. The majority of the students were at least two grades below norm and numbered about one hundred students for each grade level. The stated primary purpose of the event was to compare the impact of performance- contracting education with the impact of normal education received by underachieving children so a similar group of students (control group) in traditional classrooms were selected and tested. Several existing school programs already included remedial classes in their repertoire, and these went on as usual. Altogether, more than 27,000 children took part in the project with about 10,800 involved in programs offered by private firms, 11,880 in the control group, 1,000 in special programs and 1,080 being a part of a contract between two districts and their teachers' groups. With as broad a scope as this study included, naturally, there were many educators anxious to scrutinize the results. The experiment was also significant because it began a virtual trend toward performance contracting in the USA. Typical of the procedure by which to negotiate a performance contract were those initially outlined by a firm known as Educational Turnkey Systems Inc. of Washington, D.C. They recommended that the following steps be taken:

1. The school system should consult with parents, teachers and administrators regarding the present instructional program.
2. The school should then ascertain the program's weaknesses and determine the needs to be met by the industry to be contacted.
3. The school should submit a "request for proposal" to several different private companies, specifying the performance levels expected, payment to be made for the various people to be hired, and then approach a selected firm(s) for negotiation.
4. The contractors would respond by bidding on requested programs offering certain guarantees and with appended cost effectiveness estimates. They would also propose a specific instructional program.
5. The school would enlist a "management support

group, another independent party with knowledge of the industry to help analyze the program and to select personnel.

6. The school would hire a private educator to monitor on a continual basis the success of the contractor's program. It should be noted that the school system's staff, administrators, trustees and community should be actively participating in the program and monitoring it according to available information.

7. If the program was considered successful at the completion of an agreed upon demonstration period, the performance contractor could agree to extend the guarantee to the entire school system at the same rate of pay.

8. The local educational authority, with a management support group would then "turnkey" the contractor's instructional program into the system and the system would take over the process.

A serious complaint of the performance contracting movement occurred with regard to testing and skill maintenance. Some doubted that proper testing of skill attainment could really be accomplished and others warned that if results were indeed positive there was no assurance that these would be maintained by the student for any significant length of time. In fact, in one of the early contracts negotiated with the Dorsett Educational Systems, Inc., the public trustees neglected to work in just such a clause. Later, they realized that it might have been beneficial to prescribe penalties to the company if initial gains in skills disappeared after a six month period.[40] By the second year of the experiment, formal evaluations were in full swing and the "fur flew" in terms of detecting deficiencies in the operation. Chiefly targeted were such items as not using appropriate tests; failure to obtain the services of a reliable support group, i.e. people who could handle such items as requests for additional monies, draw up appropriate proposals and monitor the program; and convincing school board members, administrators and teachers that the project was viable and legitimate. One school board president who became an early convert to performance contracting worked on her reluctant peers by selecting the most influential people on the board and assigning them the task of studying contracts and reporting back to the board. The tactic apparently worked very well.[41]

Clouds of doubt that soon appeared over the Texarcana experiment specifically also involved some very serious

110

accusations. Companies on contract were accused of "teaching to the test" and neglecting student needs. The president of one such company involved, Lloyd G. Dorsett, suggested that this contamination had occurred due to an overzealous programmer cramming too much work into too short a period. Texarcana School Superintendent, Edward D. Trice, countered with the statement that the assertion that any teaching to a test was not good pedagogy.[42] And so the debate went on.

## Analysis

There are at least two things of concern in assessing the performance contracting movement, the first of which is the pervasive myth that things can usually be solved by turning them over to the "know-how" world of business and industry. Although the failure of this practice has been documented with regard to other attempts to manage the educational enterprise scientifically, the belief still lingers.[43] The second unfortunate fallacy is that suggestions for remedying educational ills can pretty well originate in any sector other than that of the teaching profession. It is sometimes ironic that a society that pays such easy heed to professionals in any other field seems to think that when it comes to the education of their offspring, they or any elected official or even business-minded individual is more qualified or more likely to offer valid advice.

By 1973 the American educational world was ready to admit that performance contracting was under serious investigation, mainly because of the difficulty it had in defining objectives in subject matter other than those involving simple skills or, in some cases difficulties in measuring the attainment of those objectives.[44] The problem, of course, has to do with the human enterprise which is so centrally connected to imperfections, emotions and perceptions. Its intricasies are so complex that even the best trained educators are willing to admit that a professional team approach is required to properly execute its requirements - counsellors, administrators, methodologists and even community workers. It would be safe to venture a guess that if an experiment was tried that would test the hypothesis that educators make the best educators, it might not only be a first in North American history, it would also constitute a first instance in education of putting the horse before the cart.

Performance contracting enthusiasts have frequently voiced their disdain with teachers and educational administrators for not supporting a development that virtually wrests authority from one nonprofessional agency (trustees) to another (private business) without their having been seriously consulted. Teachers are frequently viewed as dispensable items in the list of educational essentials, and rare is the educational reformer who has proposed alleviating this shortcoming. To a certain extent teachers themselves have been to blame because they have taken this form of professional abuse without getting very agitated about it. The fact that the profession can exert sizable influence may be concluded from the ways in which they have been able to tender effective opposition to such schemes as performance contracting and the voucher system. Justifiably, they have opposed proposals that would distract their attention from the mandate of seeking to meet the needs of individual students by substituting "performance at all costs". Perhaps what is needed now is for North American teachers to rally behind a reform plan that would give them the credit they deserve, one that would properly reflect the gradual coming of age of the profession, and would call on both their creative juices and experience as educators. It is a plan of educational reform for teachers in that sense, but it would also offer real hope for any educator because it would be steered by those who know the process best. In fact, it would improve the very process itself.

## FOOTNOTES

[1] A case in point was the Social Credit party cry in Alberta for the development of a voucher system in the province. The underlying argument was that vouchers would produce higher standards of education through competition between schools. Parents would have a greater say in the education of their children and assure that the people best qualified to decide about such things, namely parents, would be in control. Lawrence Martin, "Socreds Push for Vouchers", ATA News, Vol. 15, No. 17, May 19, 1981, 1-2.

[2] David G. Young, Educational Vouchers: Boon or Bane, Edmonton: Government of Alberta, Department of Educational Planning and Research Branch, July 1981, 35 pp.

[3] Laura Salganik, "The Rise and Fall of Educational Vouchers", Education Digest, December 1981, 6-9.

[4] David G. Young, Educational Vouchers, 4.

[5] Ibid., 6-7.

[6] Ibid., 14-17.

[7]R. Freeman Butts, "Educational Vouchers: The Private Pursuit of the Public Purse", Phi Delta Kappan, Vol. 61, No. 1, September 1979, 7-8.

[8]John E. Coons, "Of Family Choice and Public Education", Phi Delta Kappan, Vol. 61, No. 1, September 1979, 10-13, and D. Stephen Sugarman, "Family Choice in Education", Oxford Review of Education, Vol. 6, No. 1, 1980, 31-40.

[9]Hubert S. Szanto, "California's Voucher Plan: A Private School Principal's Critique", NASSP Bulletin, Vol. 64, September 1980, 93-98.

[10]John E. Coons, "Of Family Choice and 'Public' Education".

[11]Stephen D. Sugarman, "Family Choice in Education".

[12]Tony W. Johnson, "Educational Vouchers: An Idea Whose Time Has Come", USA Today, Vol. 110, May 1982, 27-29.

[13]"Tuition Tax Credits: The President's Proposal", American Education, Vol. 18, No. 4, May 1982, 16-19.

[14]Ibid.

[15]Anne Graham, "Joining the Discussion: Tuition Tax Credits", American Education, Vol. 18, No. 6, July 1982, 13-15.

[16]Robert B. Hawkins, Jr., "Tuition Tax Credits: Another Voice", American Education, Vol. 18, No. 8, October 1982, 9-10.

[17]Ibid.

[18]E.G. West, "Tuition Tax Credits: Equity Issues", American Education, Vol. 19, No. 6, July 1983, 12-15.

[19]Robert E. Baldwin, "Freedom of Choice in Education", American Education, Vol. 18, No. 7, August-September 1982, 17-23.

[20]Thomas Sowell, "Tuition Tax Credits: A Social Revolution", American Education, Vol. 18, No. 6, July 1982, 18-19.

[21]Sister Rennee Oliver, O.S.U., "Tuition Tax Credits

and The Poor", American Education, Vol. 61, No. 6, July 1983, 13, 16.

[22]Ibid., 13.

[23]James S. Catterall and Henry M. Levin, "Public and Private Schools: Evidence on Tuition Tax Credits", Sociology of Education, Vol. 55, April/July 1982, 144-151.

[24]Anne Graham, "Joining the Discussion".

[25]D.A. Erikson, "Should All The Nation's Schools Compete For Clients And Support?" Phi Delta Kappan, Vol. 61, No. 1, September 1979, 14-17.

[26]J. Lawrence McConville, "Evolution of Performance Contracting", Educational Forum, Vol. 37, May 1973, 443-452.

[27]J.A. Mecklenburger, "Performance Contracting: One View", Educational Leadership, Vol. 29, January 1972, 297-300.

[28]Martin Reed, "Performance Contracting: Did We Learn Anything?" American School Board Journal, Vol. 159, May 1972, 30-32.

[29]Leon M. Lassinger, "Input", Instructor, Vol. 80, June/July 1971, 19-20.

[30]William Dickinson, Ed., Performance Contracting: A Guide for School Board Members and Community Leaders, Evanston, Ill.: National School Board Association, 1971, 67.

[31]Thomas A. Shannon, "Why Schools Aren't Businesses", American School Board Journal, Vol. 67, No. 1, June 1980, 29-30.

[32]James A. Mecklenburger, "Performance Contracts: One View", 297.

[33]Charles Blaschke, "From Gold Stars to Green Stamps", Nation's Schools, Vol. 88, No. 3, September 1971, 51-52.

[34]Ibid., 53.

[35]Reed Martin and Charles Blaschke, "Contracting for Educational Reform", Phi Delta Kappan, Vol. 52, March 1971, 403-405.

[36] Myron H. Dembo and Donald A. Wilson, "A Performance Contract in Speed Reading", Journal of Reading, Vol. 16, May 1973, 627-633.

[37] Ibid., 632.

[38] "The Customers Pass the Test - or Else", Business Week, Vol. 42, September 1970, 42, 46.

[39] Albert H. Yee, "The Limits of Scientific-Economic-Technological Approaches and the Search for Perspective in Education: The Case for Performance Contracting", The Journal of Educational Research, Vol. 66, No. 1, September 1972, 19-29.

[40] Stanley Elam, "The Age of Accountability Dawns in Texarcana", Phi Delta Kappan, Vol. 52, June 1970, 509-512.

[41] "Texarcana: The second year around", Nation's Schools, Vol. 87, March 1971, 32-33.

[42] "Clouds and Controversy over Texarcana", Nation's Schools, Vol. 86, October 1970, 85-86, 88.

[43] Daniel Tanner, "Performance Contracting: Contrivance of the Industrial-Governmental-Educational Complex", Intellect, Vol. 101, March 1973, 361-365.

[44] P. Carpenter and G.R. Hall, Case Studies in Educational Performance Contracting, Vol. I: Conclusions and Implications, Santa Monica, Calif.: Rand Corporation, 1971, ix.

## Chapter Six

## SCHOOL REFORM FOR TEACHERS: CAN WE PLAY TOO?

By now most people are aware that changing social and economic conditions have drastically affected the teacher's role in the last century. The result has reverberated in a series of amendments to the way teachers perform today, both personally and professionally. Teachers can proudly point to the fact that the restricting conditions of the past will probably never again be imposed on members of the profession, e.g. not the rigid rules to be adhered to in a 1922 teaching contract when the wages were only $75.00 per month. Teachers were:

1. Never to get married. The contract becomes null and void immediately if the teacher gets married.

2. Not to keep company with men.

3. Not to loiter in ice cream stores.

4. Not to leave town without the permission of the chairman of the school board.

5. Not to smoke cigarettes.

6. Not to dye her hair.

7. Not to wear dresses more than two inches above the ankles.

8. Not to ride in a carriage with any man other than her father or brother.

9. To keep the classroom clean by sweeping it daily; and

10. Not to wear face powder, mascara and lipstick.[1]

It might be argued that the pay cheque of the twenties decade was probably comparable to that of other similar professionals, but the rules relating to personal conduct were certainly "extraordinary" in terms of their severity.

Some school districts sixty years ago took it upon themselves to have teachers sign statements outlining their personal conduct in some quite sensitive areas. Note, for example, the following illustrative excerpts from a teacher-school board contract from that time period:

I promise to take a vital interest in all phases of Sunday-school work, donating my time, service and money without stint for the uplift and benefit of the community.

I promise to abstain from all dancing, immodest dressing, and any other conduct unbecoming a teacher and a lady.

I promise not to encourage or tolerate the least familiarity on the part of any of my boy pupils.

I promise to sleep at least eight hours a night, to eat carefully, and to take every precaution to keep in the best of health and spirits in order that I may better be able to render efficient service to my pupils.

I promise to remember that I owe a duty to the townspeople who are paying me my wages, that I owe respect to the school board and the superintendent that hired me, and that I shall consider myself at all times the willing servant of the school board and the townspeople.[2]

The servanthood concept of teaching was evident in a variety of ways. In Lower Canada, Jean-Baptiste Meilleur, who became the first superintendent of education for that region of the country, recommended that teachers cultivate land or a garden as a source of profit to supplement their wages. This would further set a positive example for the children as well as give them the opportunity to learn good work habits under the tutelage of their teachers. Further, teachers were required to "board around" in various homes and thus give the families whose homes they occupied an additional advantage in that they could be tutored by their resident teacher in acquiring the three "R's". They might read to the family, instruct those who were willing, or even provide special lessons to the children.[3] In the State of Vermont, where this practice was also quite commonplace, sixty-eight percent of all teachers were occupied thusly in 1862. In Connecticut, there were eight-four percent so involved in 1846. One of the factors undoubtedly contributing to the eventual demise of the practice was the gradual realization that teachers had no private lives of their own.

The sexist nature of the teacher's image in the early part of this century is underscored in the practice of conceiving of the job as a feminine role. This view has prevailed for a number of decades, and is partially fuelled by fact that a large number of women enter the profession. About two-thirds of teachers are women, many of whom see the profession as a temporary occupation. A much higher percentage of women engaged in teaching today marry than was the case in the 1930's, but even now they consider their occupation as ancillary to that of their husbands. It is still true as well that many women leave teaching to have children and never return to the classroom. Finally, until recently, many teachers, both men and women, who started out in the profession left within a few years of entering it, thus adding evidence to the view that teaching was primarily women's work, and if men did enter it, it was only until they found something else. Recent economic constraints have changed that trend, although the number of males in teaching has also risen over the years.

Sexism can hinder a profession if equality is unjustly available to either gender. For the most part, the male teacher has traditionally had the advantage in teaching, although the picture is changing. As the quest for equality of regard in society generally mounts, women are slowly being awarded the just due for their efforts in the various sectors.

In the teaching profession of a half century ago men did not necessarily escape the rigor of moral scrutiny cast upon them. In one instance a young male teacher created a near scandal when he was seen walking in public with a female companion. He chose to fight against his critics by addressing a letter to the New York Teacher in which he demanded respect for his private rights as a citizen. "I am a citizen," he said, "and I shall exercise the immunities of citizenship as I deem proper, the whole town of L____ notwithstanding." If the young lady in question had designs on the young man in question, she got an assist from the editor who advised him to take a fast walk with her - down the aisle to the altar.[4]

## THE EMERGING PROFESSION

The fact that the educational enterprise is replete with interest groups of various kinds as well as several deserving of professional consideration - teachers and administrators - often allows for no clear lines of authority or control to emerge. Two basic factors have aided greatly in the growth of the teaching profession to its present status, however, and supported their claim to greater authority in schooling. The first is the fact of their enhanced education and the second, that of increased awareness of self-image which was partially motivated by the proliferation of teacher organizations and/or unions.

## Teacher Education

The first normal school in North America was opened in Montreal in 1836, three years before Horace Mann established the first State Normal School in the United States at Lexington, Massachusetts. This move was further fueled by such educational leaders as Egerton Ryerson and Marshall D'Avary in eastern Canada, and by 1855 there were such institutions in Nova Scotia, 1856 in Prince Edward Island, and 1857 in Newfoundland.

The initial one year normal school program consisted of a smattering of all subject matters that would be taught in school as well as a little methodology, with the main objective of trying to turn sixteen to eighteen year old adolescents into educational technicians in a very short period of time. Furthermore, anyone attempting to complete the program was virtually guaranteed success, both academically as well as in terms of getting a position. In the four year period, 1919-1923 at the Calgary Normal School, out of a total of 910 students, two failed, and seven withdrew, not necessarily because they were doing failing work.[5] In comparison with other professions, of course, teachers fared quite well in terms of the actual amount of time spent in formal training, but the manner in which the community was oriented to receiving teachers left something to be desired. Many viewed teachers as youth who required assistance with the raising of the community's children, some of whom required a little raising themselves.

The Canadian shift away from Normal School training was partially influenced by an American trend towards the teachers college. By 1900, a two year program of studies was required in many states and by 1905 the Michigan and Albany Normal Schools had been granted the status of state colleges and conferred their first bachelor degrees in teaching. By 1921, forty-two percent of the United States Normal Schools or Teachers' Colleges were granting degrees.[6] This development was a bit slower in Canada with the first university programs in teacher education originating in Ontario and Saskatchewan in the early twenties. The University of Alberta followed in 1929 by establishing a School of Education within the Faculty of Arts and Sciences and later becoming the first university to incorporate all aspects of teacher training within the confines of university jurisdiction (in 1941).   Newfoundland became the second province to do so in 1949.

The content of teacher training programs today vary little from the initial format adopted some forty years ago, and this factor should silence the critics who insist that the profession either lacks a sense of disciplinary direction or academic consistency.   M.E. LaZerte's program at the University of Alberta, for example, consisted of four components, smacking heavily of a familiar social science base.   The first was educational psychology, including statistics, especially interpretive tests, with much outside reading required of students.   Second, was history and philosophy of education stressing the development of the attitudes of openmindedness and healthy skepticism.   Third, was educational administration which included more pedestrian activities such as timetabling, school law, classroom management and teachers' organizations, and finally, there was the science and practice of teaching.   For almost the whole academic year students spent two days a week in the classroom, at first in junior high schools and later in the high schools.   Students were required to be familiar with all of the subjects being taught and were required to have a prepared lesson plan for every lesson they were assigned. Although there were problems of supervision due to a lack of adequate number of faculty available, the curriculum was rigorously adhered to and the student's performance strictly evaluated.[7]

An examination of current university programs leading to the Bachelor of Education degree, particularly in the West, reveals a remarkable similarity to LaZerte's program. Educational administration, teaching methodology, educational foundations and psychology are all vital aspects of the program.   There may be more options available, e.g. early childhood major or English as a second language, etc., but the emphasis on gaining adequate classroom experience for the would-be teacher is still a primary concern.   Logically, the evidence leads to the conclusion that the academic basis of teacher education not only rests of a long history in North America, but easily boasts as solid a scientific base as any other profession.

Teacher Organizations

The teacher movement to organizing professionally began in Prince Edward Island in 1840 via the Society of Schoolmasters and the Association des Instituteurs de Montreal in 1846.   The Ontario Association developed from the Teachers' Association of Canada West formed in 1861.   Other

120

provinces followed with the later ones being the Manitoba Education Association in 1909 and the Alberta Teachers' Alliance in 1916. British Columbia had no such body prior to World War I, although its teachers met in regional institutes.[8]

Public concepts of unionization among teachers have usually been negative, partially because of the well publicized notion that professional people are somehow beyond the shallow bargaining process. John W. Barnett, originator of the Alberta movement, saw the concept as two-pronged. On the one hand he was prepared to endorse unionized kinds of tactics to catch the public eye and thus to draw attention to teacher needs while on the other hand he often chided teachers for their lack of professionalism.[9] The new militancy that pervaded teacher ranks after the First World War similarly placed great emphasis on material comforts such as salary increases, security of tenure, retirement pensions and a say in the decision-making process, while at the same time making claims about being truly professional in regard to classroom management and student care. In 1920, the Canadian Teachers' Federation came into being with chapters readily formed in the various provinces. At first, membership was voluntary, but as teachers came to recognize the need for and benefits of corporate action, the movement grew. Eventually, through the efforts of the organization and its provincial counterparts, teachers could gain title to a number of professional responsibilities which they had previously been denied. These include: curriculum-making and revision, input to teacher training, inservice education, and submissions to government through their various organizations. In a practical sense, it could be said that the teaching profession has made very great strides toward the incorporation of full professional responsibilities, and with a little extra maneuvering of the public vision, may be granted that extra push to culminate its long struggle for proper recognition.

Determining Professionalism

Through the years the teaching profession has had to wrestle with the criticism that it has not always attracted the best students to the profession, it has lacked autonomy because teachers have merely had to carry out orders originated by administrators, and it has emphasized material gain at the expense of pedagogical excellence.[10] Myron Lieberman thirty years ago noted that teachers had fallen short in achieving the measure of recognition they deserved mainly because of their lack of professional autonomy. He suggested that "... disagreement over the functions of

121

education are paralleled by disagreement over the nature of the teacher's expert authority." Still, he consoled teachers by suggesting that there were certain things which could definitely be decided by educators if they were a professional group. The list included curriculum selection, determining admission standards, qualifications for teacher training, standards of professional conduct and determining who should speak for the profession of government and to the public.[11]

In order to make a stronger case for Lieberman's argument, it might be well to point out that the requirements he outlined have virtually all been met by the teaching profession. It has surpassed the status of a "semi-profession" for example, as noted by Robert Howsam and associates. They suggest that the characteristics of a semi-profession are these:

1. Lower in occupational status.

2. Shorter training periods.

3. Lack of societal acceptance that the nature of the service and/or the level of expertise justifies the autonomy which is granted to the profession.

4. A less specialized and less highly developed body of knowledge and sills.

5. Markedly less emphasis on theoretical and conceptual bases for practice.

6. A tendency for the professional to identify with the employment institution more and with the profession less.

7. More subject to administrative and supervisory surveillance and control.

8. Less autonomy in professional decision-making with accountability to superiors rather than to the profession.

9. Management of organizations within which semi-professionals are employed by persons who have themselves been prepared and served in that semi-profession.

10. A preponderance of women.

11. Absence of the rights of privileged communication between client and professional; and

12. Little or no involvement in matters of life and death.[12]

By contrast, there are a number of criteria by which to judge whether or not a particular group qualifies as a profession, some of which are the reverse of the points mentioned above, and most if not all of which have or are being met by the teaching profession.

1. A unique attitude toward one's work including a striving for excellence, the appreciation of accomplishment above monetary rewards, and a concern for the welfare of the client and the community as a whole.
2. A theoretical base for operation rather than merely a technical one making the processes of analyses, interpretation and judgement essential.
3. The services rendered are considered unique, definite and essential by society.
4. A long period of specialized training is required which, in the case of teaching, is rapidly being expanded to five years either by virtue of specialization or additional graduate training. Implied also is the concept of continuous learning in that there is a concerted effort to keep abreast of new developments in the field.
5. An acceptance of responsibility for action and behavior. This usually involves the maintenance of a code of ethics which is adhered to by members of the profession and by which infractions are noted by the profession itself.
6. Rigorous selection of would-be entrants to the program of training. In education this applies to both initial admission to a Faculty for preparatory study as well as the issuance of a final certificate of operation.
7. A considerable degree of autonomy insofar as decision-making authority is concerned. Professional groups often monitor their own activities rather than having outsiders set policies and enforce adherence to standards.[13]

The last of the above criteria is perhaps the most distressing to teachers who aspire to an enhanced professional role for themselves, and the dilemma is intensified by the fact that aspects of educational policy and practice are overseen by several different kinds of interest groups - elected government leaders whose basis orientation is to please their constituents, members of the Department of Education who aspire to function with a minimal upheaval of any kind, members of boards of trustees who, for a variety of reasons, aspire to that office and when elected often take themselves too seriously, and administrators who sometimes tend to take direction from elected boards instead of following the dictates of their own professional training and experience. What is left in the hopper for teacher policy-making are often the scrapings that apply only to such internal matters as classroom conduct or local school operations.

To what extent are the other criteria of professional behavior dependent on decision-making opportunity? If teachers _were_ granted additional decision-making opportunities, would they grasp them with enthusiasm and vigor? Would they be able to demonstrate to the satisfaction of the community the degree of accountability that would be expected? Will teacher accountability be as reliably assured if some of the current constraints of amenability are removed? Richard Pratte suggests that teacher accountability exists on three fronts - logically, as relates to the canons of logical inquiry; strategically, as relates to technique and the execution of the teacher role; and, institutionally, as relates to the requirements of the various levels of the institution - administration, community and government.[14] Thus, is it not simply a matter of being accountable per se because accountability is also directional. Pratte does not deal with the question of personal accountability in a professional sense - only in terms of the accountability one naturally owes to truth - and thus avoids the problematic area of motivation. Would a teacher function "better" and more professionally if he/she was aware of being personally responsible for the quality of the educational enterprise? As the situation now stands, the blame for error, etc. can be significantly shifted in the direction of non-educator policy-makers, thereby affording the teacher both an "out" and a missed opportunity in a vital area of potential growth.

Before the teaching profession will culminate its quest for total professionalism, their own members will first have to address the issue of how much this quest is desired. Likely they will need to develop an enhanced self-image that will reflect confidence in themselves as professionals, and then be ready to measure up to any test of that integrity.[15] Teachers will also need to formulate a means by which the rigor of the profession is maintained, perhaps by avoiding the tendency to produce as many teachers as the market demands following a philosophy which incorporates quality rather than quantity of product. The viewpoint that it is always better to have someone in the classroom labelled a teacher, albeit a poorly and inadequately trained person, than to have the school unavailable has mitigated against any significant[16] sustained improvement in the quality of teacher preparation. That "need", too, will have to be addressed by members of the profession.

David Flower of the Alberta Teachers Association has suggested that all professions be treated alike, and he has lambasted the Alberta Government for seeking to undermine the teaching profession by eliminating negotiated rights of the past with regard to the development of a new Teaching Professional Act. While the government has allowed other professions such as accountants and psychologists to monitor their own professional affairs, the Minister of Education has appeared to be quite adamant about reneging on such a right for teachers. In his view, "The teaching profession is not[17] exactly like other professions." In truth, no two are exactly alike.

It is not only governments who need to acknowledge the transformation of the teaching profession from a fledgling group of semi-trained country girls and boys to the scientifically monitored human enterprise that it is today. The public, too, will need to be enlightened. This will no doubt come about much quicker when teachers begin to appreciate the advantages of increased autonomy in educational operations and work toward that attainment. An initial step would be to unclutter the arena of educational governance to make way for a less inhibited display of professional competence.

## GOVERNANCE OF EDUCATION

Education is big business in Canada with some 5,685,680 Canadians, slightly less than a quarter of the population, enrolled fulltime in Canada's 30.2 billion dollar educational enterprise during 1983-84. Of this number, 4,949,660 students were from the elementary and secondary schools enrolled in 14,000 schools.[18]

Naturally, such an industry has multiple numbers of groups involved in its organization and process, and in the case of schooling this includes the federal government, provincial and territorial governments through their departments of education, elected school boards, school superintendents and principals, teachers, P.T.A. and other community groups, and last, but not least, the students. The role of the federal government is easily delineated since its involvement in education is minimal. Except for the education of Status Indians and Inuit, children of the military and penitentiary inmates, the federal government is basically a funding agency with jurisdiction for the enterprise turned over to the provinces. Corollary assistance is also available for such programs as the Official Languages Program and those offered through the Multiculturalism Directorate of the Secretary of State Department, but direct supervision of these programs is assigned to local bodies or branches.

## Educational Partners

Foremost on the educational scene insofar as jurisdiction is concerned are the provincial departments of education. Basically, the resemblance between the various provincial departments is significant, comprising a structure including the Minister responsible (an elected official), deputy minister(s), and a host of civil servants who fulfill a variety of functions pertaining to curriculum-making, evaluation, and testing. In many cases, teachers and administrators are called on to have input to the activities of curriculum and test making via committees that serve to perform specialized tasks. In addition, governments sometimes set up commissions to study aspects of the educational enterprise, the basis of which often become the ground on which reforms are based. It is sometimes suggested that civil servants have a greater say in the operations of education than elected officials do, but if this has indeed occurred, the means exist by which it can be corrected by the Minister or other elected members merely by laying claim to the democratic rights attributed them by the body politik.

Many people regard school boards (or trustee boards) to be an added guarantee of democracy at the local level, although school boards are created strictly through the provisions of provincial School Acts. Originally, the B.N.A. Act, Section 93, included four subsections to guarantee the existence of local school boards, but the current interpretation is that a province may choose to delegate certain of its powers to local jurisdictions. There is nothing either sacred nor logistical in current Canadian law to guarantee the formation of school boards, and they have actually outlived their usefulness as a further democratic safeguard. Generally speaking, the degree of control of school boards varies a little throughout the country, but essentially they are charged with providing: (i) a full range of educational programs, (ii) qualified personnel to man these programs, (iii) buildings and facilities suitable for operating these programs, and (iv) an equitable distribution of grant monies.[19]

As a specific example, in Alberta, school boards are delegated to: (i) assume responsibility for the administration and provision of educational services, (ii) contribute to the formation of educational policy, (iii) apply grant monies to designated areas of service, and (iv) recognize the role of parents, community[20] and students in the utilization of educational services.

Parental input into education has usually been viewed as a vital part of the educational process from the original arrangement that any parent in prairie days might wish to spend an hour in the schoolhouse telling the teacher off to the sophisticated machinery of a well-oiled P.T.A. or parent advisory council. More recently room has been made on the agenda to listen to student concerns, although too often these have been limited to more pedantic matters pertaining to the designation of smoking areas, whether or not to run in hallways, or the supply and location of lockers. As students become more sophisticated in utilizing their strengths in the ongoings of the democratic process, they may also wish to exalt the academic calibre of their list of demands.

The issue of educational governance often brings up the question of authority versus control, with the former referring to the legal aspect of the question and the matter of control being more aligned with realia. In America, a persistent fear is that government will adopt an increasingly heavy hand in the institution, as Jack Schuster has stated, "There has been no shortage of state politicians and education department officials decrying excessive federal regulation ..."[21] Stephen Arons echoes this fear adding that the educational enterprise cannot be a proper function of government, whether that government be democratic or not.[22] Who then is to govern schooling? Since the intent of basic education is often taken to be the informing of children about the basic values of society, governments often take this as a legitimate rationale to "take charge" of the operation so that those sacred entities will be preserved. Jeffrey Kane assures Americans that this is a futile effort on the part of the government as history has recorded, since the school cannot be used as a means to manipulate individual conscience or to recreate society.[23] Kane's argument notwithstanding, the truth is that governments throughout the history of public education have indeed tried to maneuver the school system to influence children into respecting the regimes in power, but the extent to which they have been successful is debatable, and may be a ripe field for educational historians to explore further. By contrast, in Canada, it is the role of the local which is in need of analysis and perhaps dismantling if the following examples are any indication. A Quebec White Paper issued in 1982 suggested that "school boards are viewed with anxiety, doubt and criticism". The Report recommended that school boards either be abolished or at least partially replaced with appointed officials.[24] In British Columbia recently, the Minister of Education took the granted powers away from a city school board on the grounds that they were not acting responsibly and the courts subsequently upheld his action. In Alberta, the Minister intervened in a school closure action by a city school board and warned that he would disband the board if their internal bickerings did not cease.[25] If we have anything to fear from government in public education in Canada, it would appear to emanate from the local levels, not national or provincial. It would only be fair to mention, however, that the existence of a Federal Department of Education in the U.S.A. probably emphasizes that government's role to a greater extent than is the case in Canada.

## THE CONCEPT OF SCHOOL TRUSTEE

Local governance of education by elected school board trustees is a North American tradition, not usually identifiable in any other country. The arrangement has a long history and is closely associated with notions of the desirability of local control wherever possible. It is a somewhat unusual political system (which attests also to its questionability) and yet is a vital aspect of the North American educational enterprise.

### A Brief History of the Trustee Model

The origins of school boards have to do with the assumption that government should be decentralized, and local communities should be better able to manage immediate affairs than those more distantly removed. The original authority for school boards was delegated by statute, interpreted by the courts, in some cases, expanded by custom. School board members were expected to become promoters of public interest in education, defenders and upholders of accepted values of the community, an appellate body to hear complaints and grievances, promoters of individual rights and interests, and supervisors of professional personnel.[26] In reference to the last responsibility, members of school boards have

128

sometimes taken themselves too seriously and allowed their concept of their protectionist role to infringe on the duties of professional personnel. One need not look far in identifying examples of this orientation even in today's systems. If anything, it is a growing phenomenon.

The Canadian tradition of electing school boards grew from the British tradition of freedom mingled with the Loyalist penchant for township and local townhouse meetings. By 1816, arrangements were made to have trustees for schools in upper Canada in districts having at least twenty pupils. In the West a School Ordinance was passed in 1884 which provided for the establishment of both protestant and separate schools with subsequent legislation delineating the role of school boards. [27]The action immediately affected sixty-five school districts.

The gamut of concerns for school trustees has traditionally been quite wide, i.e. finances, curriculum, school personnel, etc. This, perhaps, is the way the public has always viewed the office, but a poll published in the Phi Delta Kappan suggests that people envisage that trustees should currently be concerned with: (i) Discipline, (ii) Integration, (iii) Finance, and (iv) teachers. A survey in Ontario, however, revealed these concerns for trustees: (i) curriculum[28] (ii) teaching, (iii) teachers, and (iv) facilities. The American preference tends toward practical concerns, particularly in-school matters, while the Canadian version is more professionally oriented in terms of such items as the curriculum or the function of teachers. If present trends continue, we shall see an increase of trustee involvement in areas heretofore not assigned them. This trend fails to take cognizance of the increased capabilities of the teaching profession in such areas and effectively veers the position of trustee off its historical course of "minding the store on behalf of the local community."

Evaluating Trusteeship

The concept of trusteeship or school boards is much a product of its times of origin. In those days limited transportation and primitive means of communication made local government a virtual necessity for the purposes of proper presentation, and made this form of local responsibility a good idea. Moreover, the concept of public schooling was also in its infant stages, and it was appropriate that the community work together, especially through locally-designated officials, such as trustees, to accomplish the objectives of the newly established institution. Teachers as well were new to the process, and hardly better educated than most members of the community and the two groups often worked together as a means of launching an enterprise that would eventually take on very complicated and intricate proportions hardly envisaged by the originators of the idea.

Much time has passed since the inception of public schooling in North America, and while trustees have remained virtually untouched in their qualifications for office, their assigned (or envisaged) responsibilities have been dramatically transformed. Educators, in the meantime, have seen their study area expand immensely, particularly through advances made via the social sciences, but also in terms of related fields such as curriculum formation, evaluation and in teaching techniques. The teacher of today is a professional in that sense, having spent a considerable amount of training in a bona fide discipline, learning to comprehend the various facts and theories that make up the process of learning. In the meantime, the trustee is essentially still the same person he always was - a citizen with a yen to get involved in schooling for whatever reason, and so do his democratic duty. In fact, there is reason to suggest that the publicly-stated reasons for running for such office are quite admirable. In a survey of ninety Ottawa-Carleton candidates who ran for office in 1978 and 1980, most new candidates suggested that they were deeply concerned with what they perceived to be impersonal community relations, a lack of response to their genuine concerns, and the many difficulties which they experiences in their attempts to deal with large, impersonal, autocratic and bureaucratic school systems in general, and the school boards' appointed officials in particular.[29]

Whether the school trustee becomes disillusioned with his lack of success in accomplishing the goals he envisages for the school or simply because the pressures of the job produce it, the fact is that many trustees adopt some unusual attitudes on attaining office. Some take things personal in the sense that if their ideas are not accepted they begin a form of attack against their colleagues or against school administrators or teachers. Others begin to perceive the position as an opportunity to personally undertake a reform of the system, although their efforts are often based on good intentions or personal images rather than on professionally based procedures. This is not a day when policy-making can be relegated to good-hearted people, void of any professional knowledge, no matter how well-intentioned those would-be visionaries might be.

130

In light of the many advances made in the various fields affecting education today - pedagogy, administration, finance, etc. - it is quite foolhardy to suggest that significant responsibilities for its management should be assigned to local politicians. The democratic safeguard for the community already rests with the elected officials who make up the provincial government via the department of education. Thus there need be no fear of bypassing that honored tradition nor the meaning of the concept of democratic representation. Further, the advances rapidly being made in education quite tax the abilities of those who are operating at the very point of advance so that anyone with less knowledge would surely find himself/herself in a totally foreign context. Surely a way out of the dilemma is to afford responsibility to those who are best qualified to manage it, namely, educators instead of elected citizens.

The qualifications for school board members in an ideal sense are actually quite formidable. The nature of the task is that it is a time-consuming, thankless and demanding task that requires expertise in such matters as school finance, taxation, law, curriculum, diplomacy and public relations. The personal requirements for the role include someone who knows the difference between personal influence and factual persuasion, learns and practices the delicate art of compromise when it is necessary for progress, recognizes that not all of his votes or decisions on school policies will be popular ones, learns how to deal effectively with the news media, and accepts as a matter of course occasionally being misquoted.[30]

The practicalities of performing as a trustee or school board member imply that schools ought to be visited regularly, meetings of the board (and subcommittees) must be attended, and a series of social appearances on behalf of the school system must be undertaken. In addition, a liaison must be maintained with one's colleagues as well as the education profession, with government at local and provincial levels, with parents and a potential host of dissidents, outsiders and even pests. For all intents and purposes, schools are not usually named after board members and there is little chance that people in such office will be long remembered after they have served their terms of office. This makes the stated set of altruistic motives for service quite questionable. Unless the role is perceived to be a necessary stepping-stone to office in another realm of politics, it would be better for all if potential candidates would consider tackling the latter post directly and stay away from education altogether.

131

## Trustee Antics

Essentially, the North American concept of school trustee is based on an adversarial or confrontation model rather than being cooperation-oriented, and many novice school trustees envisage the operation of their office as "seeing to it that the teachers don't get away with too much!" In the thirties, in Alberta, school boards did everything they could to deter the practice of giving long-standing contracts to teachers, and, supported by the government of the time, lobbied to enact legislation that would give either teachers or school boards the right to terminate a contract without appeal to the board of reference. Only teachers with continuous contracts had any security of tenure and the conflict between trustees and teachers generally intensified.[31]

A long bitter teachers' strike occurred at Blairmore, Alberta in 1925, about which John Barnett, leader of the newly established Alberta Teachers' Alliance, had much to say in his organization's magazine. The school board in that town was determined to build a new school and assumed that the teachers would finance the new venture through debentures. They therefore reduced the teachers' salaries and when the proposal was refused, fired the entire staff. The teachers responded by striking, an action that officially lasted seven years and accomplished very little for the A.T.A. The provincial minister of education supported the school trustees and hired teachers with minimal qualifications to replace those who were on strike. The newly hired principal, an American, held a Montana second-class certificate.[32]

Similar attempts to deprive teachers of their legal rights were undertaken in the State of Tennessee a few years ago when the local school board successfully talked local teachers out of forming a union. The basis of their argument was amiable enough - trustees convinced the teachers that the friction produced in bargaining through union auspices would only serve to detract from the mutual advantages enjoyed by both sides in the past.[33] Still, the incident supports the contention that confrontation relations are seen by school boards as central to trustee-teacher functions.

In 1979, the city of Chicago was in financial trouble that affected all of its operations. Teachers remained unpaid for three successive pay periods, and in an effort to work themselves out of a tight squeeze, the school board devised a series of maneuvers that ultimately attracted the attention of state legislators. One of the ways in which they crawled out

132

on a financial limb was to list fake jobs in their presentation to the state for funds - a total of 3,000 jobs at $1.00 per year. Another tactic was to make their budget appear balanced by adopting a "pro-rata" line which was declared legal by the state attorney. It worked in this way: if there was a fifty million dollar deficit the board could include a minus $50 million line in the budget. They also overestimated their receivables in taxes, thereby spending money they had no hope of ever collecting.[34] While these tactics acre not intended to suggest that they represent the nature of school board operations per se, they do represent typical kinds of adversarial activities between school boards and teachers. When the Chicago board eventually hired a new superintendent to bring in a balanced budget they undercut his first recommendations by voting to exceed the spending he foresaw as a means of bringing back fiscal responsibility.

## Analysis

Although one runs the risk of being accused of reflecting personal concerns when one broaches the question of alternatives to the office of trusteeship, the case must still be made that the structure allowing for such office is obsolete. What is of greater concern, however, is that its continued maintenance hinders the development of the teaching profession by robbing the profession of opportunities for enhanced development. If we take for granted that the status quo of educational hierarchy should not be questioned we continue to operate in the muddy waters of uncertainty insofar as decision-making is concerned. After observing school boards for some time one detects a range of approaches to decision-making, primary of which is politics, namely, seeking to please as great a number of constituents as possible or even changing positions on an issue without undue concern if it is deemed to be politically advisable. Some will vote whatever way they believe their constituents would wish them to in true representative style. Others have a favorite cause which they wish to support to the exclusion of other considerations. For some, that cause is cost-cutting, at any cost, and[35] any proposal that reduces expenditures is supported. Improved educational policy, even in cases where trustees might be competent to judge such, is rarely the main objective for such functioning.

Equally important to the cost-cutting orientation among trustees is the protectionist stance of keeping additional power away from teaching staff. If, for example, the issue of teachers serving on school boards is mentioned, the argument is launched that anyone should be prohibited from engaging in decision-making bodies in respect to matters in which they have a personal economic interest.[36] Such reasoning does not take into account the numbers of corporations where presidents or executive members sit on boards which vote on such matters as personal salary increases, etc.

If cost-cutting or pleasing the constituents as a means of assuring re-election are to be considered primary philosophical premises conducive to effective trusteeship, we should indeed become fearful of any proposals to make that office into a "fulltime" position, thereby assuring even a greater devotion to politics and the continual search for newspaper headlines. In at least one Ontario study, the quest for fulltime trustees seems to emanate from large urban school board members where politics are already a big item on the local agenda.[37]

The last line of the twelfth chapter of the Bible's Book of First Corinthians which serves as a prelude to the "love" chapter suggests, "I will show you a better way", and that is what is needed in the case of the antiquated concept of school boards. Robert Patterson of the University of Alberta is not as direct, instead urging trustees to explore, to learn about learning. He suggests that it will take courage for an elected official to give his/her constituents an unpopular message, but that is the challenge for the office.[38] Proper analysis reveals, however, that the real frontier in education is to take away that "challenge" and place it in the hands of responsible, informed and professionally trained people, namely teachers. The current system tends to thwart the efforts of creative educators when trustees have to labour to understand the meaning of a proposal against their lack of pedagogical familiarity. When trustees constantly throw cold water on creative proposals for the organization (perhaps because they fail to understand its meaning or implications), new ideas seldom appear and the system retreats to a stance of organizational survival and maintenance. The same is true in regard to policy-making and school administration. Who is to administer the schools? Classically, the school board hired trained administrators for that function even though the board has the power to cancel, amend or seriously change any interpretation that administration may have of a particular policy. Boards are entrusted by the public to make "reasonable" rules, even though the nature of the process which brings them to office is based on other kinds of considerations. Logically, reasonable practices should be the expected output of people who possess the kind of knowledge and experience to function within those guidelines. That

134

criterion would seem to rule out the orbit of political wrangling.

A study of educational administration in Manitoba by Peter Coleman indicates that policy-making is viewed by school trustees as their most important function. It would seem, he suggests, that the school superintendent would logically be involved in this process since that office represents a vital source of expertise. Coleman finds, however, that this is hardly ever the case. Essentially, the superintendent's role is restricted to the implementation of policies originated by the board.[39] Our interpretation would be that eagerness to fulfill an erroneous concept of trusteeship is responsible for the practice of omitting the superintendent's input on policy-making and the way to avoid this unfortunate omission would be to assign greater direct authority to school administrators and teachers. An added benefit that accrues as a result of assigning greater decision-making opportunities to educators is a decided boost in morale that directly affects the quality of education.[40]

The 1982 White Paper on education in Quebec suggests that school boards should have their authority modified and their role and powers redefined as a "service pool" for the schools. Their responsibilities would then be limited to hiring staff, assigning students, arranging transport, deciding which optional courses would be offered, etc. The number of school boards would be reduced by half and they would be governed by an administrative council composed of one representative of each area council (about 30 people), three people designated for three years by and from the elected representatives of the regional county municipalities, and one representative appointed for three years by and from the administrators of the area's private schools. The current system of electing school trustees would be abolished.[41]

Obviously, the Quebec White Paper furnishes a step in the right direction, a step that takes cognizance of the changing educational scene in North America. It serves as an important supplement to the view of B. Levin, a former school board member, who saw that office in a realistic albeit radical fashion. His observations are that school boards (and he was once a board member) have no proper function. This is so for two reasons; first, because trustees do not truly represent their constituents; instead they sit in their boardrooms and bewail the apathy of the people. Second, schoolboards claim to make policy but what they do is discuss maintenance services and call it a policy decision. Dealing with objectives, what schools do and what kind of children they want the schools to produce are too difficult for them to handle. Yet those are questions of the first priority.[42]

Levin's observations are close to the issue of concern here. It is true that the argument of democratic representation is frequently raised insofar as trusteeship is concerned, but as we have shown, that representation is already assured by virtue of elected office in the provincial legislation. Even the original design of the office of trustee was merely to bring democracy to the local level when communications were of a much slower variety than they are today. The policy issues Levin raises serve again to support the basic contention of this thesis that there is indeed a better way. Educational policies should be made by those who understand them and who are qualified to formulate them. This clearly calls for a major reform in North American education to a system that fulfills many of the shortcomings sketched in previous chapters. It is a design that not only assures choice in schooling, and recognizes the contributions that the teaching profession can make when released from its current repertoire of encumbrances, but places educational policy-making in the hands of a different group. The arrangement will involve a significant shift in public orientation, but if introduced on a pilot basis with ample preparation and explanation, may be the most significant development in education in this century. The bottom line is that the format promises to deliver a closer facsimile of quality education than has been the case to date.

## FOOTNOTES

[1]Leo Anglin, et.al., Teaching: What It's All About. New York: Harper and Row, 1982, 194.

[2]Louis Fisher and David Schimmel, The Civil Rights of Teachers. New York: Harper and Row, 1973, 1-2.

[3]J.K. Jobling, "Jean-Baptiste Meilleur: Architect of Lower Canada's School System", in Robert S. Patterson, et.al., Profiles of Canadian Educators. Toronto: D.C. Heath, 1974, 112-113.

[4]Jean Dresden Grambs, et.al. (Eds.), Education in the World Today. Reading, Mass.: Addison-Wesley, 1972, 319.

[5]J.W. Chalmers, "Milton E. LaZerte: Consistent Professional", in R.S. Patterson, et.al., Profiles of Canadian Educators, 363-385.

[6]F. Henry Johnson, A Brief History of Canadian Education. Toronto: McGraw-Hill, 1968, 158.

[7]J.W. Chalmers, "Milton E. LaZerte", 368-369.

[8]F.Henry Johnson, A Brief History of Canadian Education, 165.

[9]J.W. Chalmers, "John W. Barnett: Organizer of Teachers", in R.S. Patterson, et.al., Profiles of Canadian Educators, 340-362.

[10]Hugh A. Stevenson, "Crisis and Continuum: Public Education in the Sixties", in J. Donald Wilson, et.al., Canadian Education: A History. Scarborough: Prentice-Hall, 1970, 500-501.

[11]Myron Lieberman, Education As A Profession. Englewood Cliffs, N.J.: Prentice-Hall, 1956, 91.

[12]Robert B. Howsam, et.al., Educating a Profession, quoted in Joseph Abruscato, Introduction to Teaching and the Study of Education. Englewood Cliffs, N.J.: 1985, 34.

[13]Other such lists are provided by Kevin Ryan and James M. Cooper, Those Who Can, Teach. Boston: Houghton-Mifflin, 1972, 300-301, and Pat Duffy Hutcheon, A Sociology of Canadian Education. Toronto: Van Nostrand Reinhold, 1975, 128-129.

[14]Richard Pratte, The Public School Movement. New York: David McKay, 1973, 154.

[15]T.E. Giles and A.J. Proudfoot, Educational Administration in Canada. Calgary: Detselig, 1984, 189.

[16]Robert S. Patterson, "History of Teacher Education in Alberta", in David C. Jones, et.al., Shaping the Schools of the Canadian West. Calgary: Detselig, 1979, 192-207.

[17]Editorial, "Why not treat all professions alike?" The ATA News, Vol. 19, No. 17, June 1985, 2.

[18]Canadian Education Association, An Overview of Canadian Education, Third Edition, CEA, 252 Bloor Street West, Toronto, 1984, 7.

[19]CEA. An Overview of Canadian Education, 24.

137

[20]Partners in Education, Proposals for Amending the School Act and Related Legislation, Government of Alberta, 1985, 23.

[21]Jack H. Schuster, "Educational Politics in a New Era", California Journal of Education, Vol. IX, Winter 1982, 1-48.

[22]Stephen Arons, Compelling Belief: The Culture of American Schooling. New York: New Press, McGraw-Hill, 1983.

[23]Jeffrey Kane, In Fear of Freedom: Public Education and Democracy in America. New York: The Myrin Institute, 1984, 6.

[24]The Quebec School: A Responsible Force in the Community, Ministere de l'Education, Gouvernement du Quebec, 1982.

[25]Calgary Herald, June 14, 1984.

[26]Keith Goldhammer, The School Board. New York: Center for Applied Research in Education, 1966, 10-14.

[27]T.C. Weidenhamer, The Alberta School Trustees Association. Edmonton: Alberta Teachers' Association, 1976, 1-6.

[28]Peter Coleman, The School Trustee and the Administration of Education. Winnipeg: The Manitoba Association of School Trustees, 1973, 412-413.

[29]Harold E. Jakes, "Why Did They Run?", Ontario Education, Vol. 15, No. 1, March/April, 1983, 18-22.

[30]George Donian, "Recognize and Acquire These Attributes as a Good School Board Member", The American School Board Journal, Vol. 168, No. 2, February 1981, 34.

[31]John W. Chalmers, Schools of the Foothills Province. Edmonton: Alberta Teachers' Association, 1967, 443.

[32]J.W. Chalmers, "John Barnett: Organizer of Teachers", 358-359.

[33]Sam P. Sentelle, "Board Talks Teachers Out of a Union", The American School Board Journal, Vol. 168, No. 7, July 1981, 38.

[34]Casey Banas, "The Chicago School Finance Catastrophe", Phi Delta Kappan, Vol. 61, No. 8, April 1980, 519-522.

[35]Lyn McLeod, "The Trustee ... A Corporate Member", Ontario Education, Vol. 15, No. 3, May/June 1983, 2-7.

[36]n.a. "Teachers Serving as Members of Board of Education - Conflict of Interest", Ontario Education, Vol. 14, No. 1, January/February, 11-15.

[37]Harold E. Jakes, "The Question of Fulltime Trustees", Ontario Education, Vol. 14, No. 2, March/April 1982, 6-10.

[38]R.S. Patterson, "The Challenge to Trustees", The Trustee, Vol. 52, No. 3, Fall 1982, 4-7.

[39]Peter Coleman, The School Trustee and the Administration of Education, 417.

[40]See chapter one in John W.Friesen, et.al., The Teacher's Voice: A Study of Teacher Participation in Educational Decision-Making in Three Alberta Communities. Lanham, MD.: University Press of America, 1983.

[41]"Quebec Publishes its 'White Paper' on School Reform", Newsletter of the Canadian Association, September 1982, 1.

[42]B. Levin, "Reform and School Trustees", in Terrence Morrison and Anthony Burton (Eds.), Options: Reforms and Alternatives for Canadian Education. Toronto: Holt, Rinehart and Winston, 1973, 302-307.

## Chapter Seven

## TOWARDS AUTONOMY:  THERE IS A BETTER WAY

Any reform plan for education must take account of its underlying purpose, namely, to educate children.  Spelled out in plain words, this means to try to afford every student an equal opportunity to develop his full potential in all aspects of living and being, and then to encourage him to make use of the developed skills/abilities in a manner that is contributory to society.  This objective applies equally to all children regardless of which end of the spectrum they represent in terms of abilities and regardless of their cultural heritage, race, creed, or religion.  This aim takes priority over all other claims on education, including trustee whims, teachers' rights or even what any given constituency may judge to be appropriate at any given time.  That much our history has established for us.

There is little doubt that many preceding educational reforms in North America have been motivated by reasons other than the child's best interests, money being one of them and politics probably running a close second.  A few plans for reform have been considered, or perhaps even inaugurated, because of strong lobbying on the part of various pressure groups.  To be properly based, however, it is mandatory that proposed educational patterns be based on sound philosophical considerations.  Strictly speaking, that criterion effectively rules out the input of those who have no familiarity with the notion of formulating basic assumptions, and for whom mere election to public office does not afford that expertise.

Philosophical Bases of Education
_____

Any reform plan for education must signify a response to the fundamental issue of determining the direction for change.  This is a return to philosophy of education, namely, which of the three major systems outlined in our original chapter - traditionalism, progressivism, or vocationalism - is to become the foundation for the system?  What kinds of concepts of truth and value or aims for education will be highlighted?  Must there be only one such frame of reference or is there room for variation or modification?  Educators will readily admit that there are several different versions of explaining how children learn and perhaps no single explanation is radically superior to any other.  An autonomous system such as the one outlined here would offer a satisfactory solution to those questions because the system guarantees standardization without any suppression of creativity or variation.  The fact that the system would offer choice would in no way diminish quality of delivery since professional management would assure it. The constituency's preference for thematic diversity could be accommodated with no loss to the essentials of literacy and socialization.

## Outline of the Plan

It might be better at the outset to suggest that the plan for autonomous education be incepted on a limited or pilot basis since it would allow evaluation and because some critics will perceive it to be somewhat radical. Essentially, the approach follows a suggestion in the Quebec White Paper referred to earlier that schools become local corporations. This would mean that schools be turned over directly to groups of teachers who would operate them in much the same way as medical clinics function. The nature of the original setup could be the subject of a debate, conference or brain-storming session, but it would not take long for groups of teachers to formulate plans about how to operate these clinics. The clinics or learning centres would adhere to the expected ground rules of education, namely, adherence to provincial curricula, certified teachers and even periodic inspection by state officials. What would be unique about the arrangement would be the autonomous functioning of the learning centres, each specializing to some extent in a given area, and perhaps even espousing a particular set of values that might deviate a little from society's norms, e.g. religious, academic, vocational, etc. It would not take long for teachers to identify with a particular institution featuring the theme they could best work with, even though most learning centres would probably continue to function in basically the same way that schools do now. Diversity of choice is probably a preference for only a small minority in society who for various reasons either believe strongly in a particular value system or who perceive that the needs of their children are not being met by current arrangements.

Administration of the new learning centres would be less structured than is presently the case because centralized offices in larger urban centres would have less responsibility as the developments of the centres increased. Groups of teachers in the learning centres would develop means by which to determine their own operations by selecting principals and other staff according to need. The traditional "downtown" offices would still be needed as a base to which to refer to matters of professional interest rather than operating strictly through the provincial Department of Education teachers' organization. Ideally, a principal would be selected by the teachers in a particular learning centre,

141

perhaps by democratic vote or via selection committee process with the final decision as to assignment taking into account the needed skills, orientation and training for such office. Eventually, the traditional title of "principal" might even disappear to be replaced by such positions as public relations teacher, facilities manager, etc. Once the new concept is introduced, there would be no need to adhere to structures based on traditional approaches.

Finances are always a concern to the educational enterprise and an autonomous arrangement would function so as to maximize individualization of each learning centre. Governments, through their departments of education, would devise an "educare" plan, similar to the medicare program with which everyone is familiar, and learning centres would draw monies from the fund on a per pupil basis similar to the way medical funds are allocated. Each child would receive the same proportion of funding and the practice of "extra billing" would have to be disallowed on the basis that it would be discriminatory. If it were exercised some learning centres would undoubtedly soon have special appeal to more enabled classes of people and thus would destroy the concept of equal opportunity as we know it. It is true that some learning centres would probably fail after a while, perhaps due to their inability to attract sufficient numbers of students; others, naturally, would do well and perhaps even develop a series of centres to form a liaison or chain of centres. Again, it is helpful to bear in mind that the atypical kinds of centres in terms of philosophy or orientation would probably have appeal to only a limited sector of the public and most schools would continue pretty much as they are now. In any event a pilot approach would be a cautious and "safe" way to begin.

Teachers who have already been told about the concept of autonomous education have shown some hesitancy in endorsing it for obvious reasons. Having been shunned in every attempt to practice their profession autonomously in the past they have also originated a less than confident concept of their success as teachers. Too many instances of failure have been generalized to suggest that "education is not doing its job, schools are worse than they have ever been, etc." Whatever the reasons, once given the opportunity to "place their abilities on the line", teachers would no doubt soon prove that they are as capable of handling their mandate to teach as other professions with equal training who "hand out their shingles" for society to utilize, e.g. psychologists, child care workers, social workers, accountants, lawyers, doctors, etc. It should be noted that many quality private schools

142

steadily play to the marketplace and fare quite well. Perhaps the greatest obstacle to overcome in this regard will be the psychological adjustment of being released from the shackles of an overzealous but uninformed group of petty politicians who take themselves too seriously. Once that yoke is taken off, the true abilities of the profession will flourish.

## Rationale for the Plan

There are a number of good reasons why an autonomous educational arrangement would be an improvement upon present schemes, the most important being that while educational standards would be maintained in such a format, the individual needs of students would be better met. Everyone knows that students learn in different ways from one another, but too often it is difficult to shift a child from a particular school when another kind of school might be helpful. Children's needs, of course, are often determined to some extent by the value system they adopt at home. Some of these do not fit into the general framework under which most schools operate and the child then functions at less than his best. For a few the option of enrolling in a private school may be feasible (financial resources permitting), and a few may select an alternative form of schooling if one is available in the system. For others, it will mean an adjustment that may never quite come off. Homogeneity in education will disallow the meeting of this need for it too frequently reflects only the whims of an absolutist state, not the vagaries of the individual child's learning habits.

A second reason for introducing autonomous education is that it more clearly reflects the nature of a pluralist society. The introduction of biculturalism/bilingualism and the later multicultural policy in Canada underscored what had been known for some time, namely, that a range of value systems exist in the country and are adhered to in ways that protect and maintain specific cultural identities without a loss of adherence to a national identity. Although only barely reflected in school policy, these concerns are a vital component of the Canadian reality. Their existence comprises a fundamental epistemological fact; to be Canadian is to have a healthy respect for diversity.

The practicalities of any assigned task in the North American tradition suggest that excellence can be attained if knowledgeability in a given area is given top priority. If learning is to be maximized and the abilities of the individual child are to be honed to their finest point, then educational policy-making and practice must be placed in the hands of

143

those who have been trained for the task in the same sense that knowledgeable doctors, lawyers and accountants are consulted for their expertise in their respective areas of knowledge. In a very real sense teachers have always performed major administrative and organizational functions within the classroom. They have made decisions about what concepts or units to teach, what textbooks or other media are to be used. Their area of responsibility needs to be expanded beyond the classroom so students will gain the added benefit of their knowledge in a greater sphere. In short, the what, how, when and where of education needs to be controlled by the profession and, like other professions, monitored through the state department as a democratic safeguard. Why should one particular profession be singled out for a double whammy of so-called democratic representation?

There is ample evidence to suggest that the move toward greater autonomy in educational decision-making would be welcomed by the public, basically because we are living in an era when expertise is both required and respected. Many families do not have the time to become versed in the rationale and mechanics of good education, and they are thus quite willing to cede operational authority to professions. Professionals also have an enormous operating advantage because they control both the stock of information about schools and about pupils. If it weren't for the cooperative mood of the teaching profession, parents would have a hard time finding out things about students or the schools that the teacher wouldn't want them to know. Also, if educational options or alternatives are to be offered there is not enough organization among consumers of education to bring such a wish to practical reality. The work place is increasingly taking time from both men and women so that the energies they might devote to the cause of their child's schooling are frequently consumed by the day-to-day rigors of the work-a-day world.[1]

The proposal to assign greater responsibility for educational delivery to teachers is also premised on the principle of the democratic rights of teachers to perform their duty. Part of being a teacher is the matter of skills, that is, those derived not only from natural ability but also honed through the appropriate training program. These skills need to be supplemented by the right to perform, not only in teaching but also in terms of corollary policy-making.[2] Too often teachers are compelled to work under unilateral patterns of leadership including conditions set by principals who perceive that teachers are subordinates or those emanating

144

from entanglements wrought by school trustees who take on more than they are elected to do. This inhibition on the profession has several noticeable effects. The teacher is frequently not given the responsibility that he/she needs to act as a professional, and second, it also discourages independent thinkers from entering the profession. Third, it depresses the atmosphere of cooperative inquiry that would have to be established if the school were to operate as a genuine centre of inquiry.[3] With an easement of these conditions, education could benefit directly from increased teacher independence.

There are few ways in which educational expertise can be better put to use than by releasing the decades of experience and knowledge pent up within the profession. Too long teachers have eaten at the trough of politics and "democratitis", the former which has seduced them into thinking that an abundance of politics is simply an evil necessity in a complex world, and the latter which has promulgated the notion that since education is "everybody's business", everybody ought to be directly involved. It is certainly true that educating children is a shared experience, but parental input can be much better implemented than through the current system of elected representative a la trusteeship. The dynamics of the situation simply call for a reallocation of input that accentuates the strengths of the teaching profession and diverts the parental role to a more productive involvement.[4]

Advantages of the Plan

The basis for any proposal to change the educational system should always be for the betterment of the child's experience in the institution. If any other cause is given priority a mesh of processes tend to entangle the network, e.g. politics. In the proposals we have examined in the previous chapters, it was shown that better education for the child has not always been the concern because various kinds of lobbyists have received too large a hearing. Also, none of the proposals have afforded attention to the teaching profession which in the intervening years has come of age. When the autonomous education plan is implemented, however, it will bring a wide range of advantages into being which will clearly affect most groups who are presently agitating for some measure of school reform.

First of all, the plan will eliminate one stage of political maneuvering and bickering as the office of trustee is abolished. This will provide the school, in the language of

145

the Quebec Report on Education, "the power to determine its
own orientations, and to plan, implement and evaluate its
educational project; in this way, it will express its real
intentions and assume its particular identity."[5]  Standards
such as use of the provincial curriculum, certification of
teachers and periodic state inspection will still be maintained,
but a significant measure of autonomy will be forthcoming so
as to enable educators to develop educational policies with
appropriate parental consultation and without interference
from trustees.

Second, the autonomous school plan will provide
significantly more choice in education and thus accommodate
the unique requirements of a wider range of students.  The
range of offerings may incorporate concerns about value
teaching, religion and cultural histories, and will stem the
tide of the growth of illegal and private schools which are
mounting rapidly in number, particularly in the West.  The
plan will also meet the requirements of a truly democratic
system in that choices will be operationalized in an accredited
setting but offering some element of variation.  If the idea of
offering variation in a school system is unsatisfactory to
today's "defenders of public education", it may be necessary
to reiterate the argument about the public's right to at least
a reasonable amount of choice, and underscore that such
choice would be controlled by certain guarantees, i.e. use of
the government-approved curriculum etc.

The third advantage has to do with finances.  The
autonomous plan would cost no more than schooling presently
does, perhaps less, because administrative services would be
decentralized.  Since each school would function on the basis
of the "marketplace" concept, it would also be easier to close
down non-producing schools rather than engage in lengthy
struggles with community groups to prolong what often turns
out to be inevitable.  Having to play to the market to some
extent would also sharpen up the offerings which the various
teacher groups would make available to the public and
challenge them to tighten up the operations of their particular
learning centre.  Budgets would also be localised in each
school thus cutting down severely on overhead costs and the
cost of allocations to the various subsection that a large
monolithic organization demands.  In other words, local
schools would need to keep a much tighter rein on spending.
Many of the administrative costs of education in larger
centres are currently connected with area offices, and layers
of superintendencies, a number of which could be eliminated
if localized control were initiated.  In Martin Mayer's
estimation,[6] in North America there are more people employed

146

in educational administration than pretty well anywhere else. Attempts to control teachers are more prevalent in the United States (and possibly Canada) than anywhere else. This plan is not intended to be an attack on school administration, but the benefits of local control and autonomy tend to parallel a diminishing of the abundance of that particular office.

The contemporary rise of interest in multiculturalism in both Canada and the United States is a positive happening insofar as the recognition of minority rights is concerned. As is evident, the movement has also developed a number of educational side-effects in that various schools for cultural and linguistic preservation have sprung up. While most of these schools have been designed to function on a part-time basis, there are also those that feature programs equal to the regular day schools. In at least a few cases, a kind of ghetto atmosphere is developed so that minority identity is highlighted above that of being one with the rest of the nation. The same may be said of some religious or value schools which function aside from the main system and thus tend to alienate their students from those who attend public schools. The autonomous plan would alleviate this tendency by assuring that even atypical schools would be typical in many respects by functioning within the general system although independent in many respects. It is important to maintain the bonds that bind the nation via the school, even though that format should also have an element of flexibility and choice built into it. If these characteristics are not allowed for, they may develop in unsatisfactory forms outside the system and work against some very basic societal goals.

## Role of Parents

The cherished notion that education is a public enterprise is strengthened through the autonomous plan for schooling in that the role of parents will be intensified. The present arrangement which includes the work of the P.T.A. and other like groups is unsatisfactory in that parental involvement is frequently limited to such areas as the purchase of school uniforms, sale of various kinds of edibles, and the sponsorship of band trips. Properly established, in the new plan each learning centre would rely heavily on the input of local parents in a variety of areas such as curriculum planning and policy formation. These aspects of the school would be more localized than is presently the case, and would reflect the combined efforts of educators and involved parents. The adversarial nature of education would be reduced if not eliminated, and teachers and parents could work cooperatively without the fear of invading each other's domain as is presently the case with trustee-teacher relations. Historically, Canadians have believed that the school should be close to the people, but current trends toward centralization and growth have worked against that realization. The autonomous plan would make localization a reality.

We are past the stage when we can say that we have community involvement because a certain percentage of parents have attended a school function. Many times it has been the only thing that parents have been allowed to do, partially because their interests are presumably covered by law via trusteeship. In an autonomous design, increased involvement would not only be welcomed, but required by virtue of the fact that many decisions and policies would reflect local needs almost entirely. Too often parent advisory councils, which are the current recognized structure to meet this need, exist in name only. Rarely do education officials really want to share basic information about the school with them.[8] Much of this orientation has been brought about by the confrontation orientation of past community-teacher relations via the office of trustee. If the parents' position on the educational landscale (not hierarchy) could be expanded to the level of a local board of education comprised of user parents, they could work much more closely with the educators who operate the local learning centre. The resultant relationship would then feature joint efforts to improve schooling because the historical-loaded point of debate - salaries - would be removed; these would be established by the local educators' group among themselves rather than by boards of education as is now the case. The central point of concentration for the joint efforts of the two parties - teachers and parents advisory council - would be the betterment of education for the children.

Getting the Word Out

The principal challenges of this model for change is the encouragement of teachers to "claim the land", and become more vocal about the accomplishments and capabilities of their profession. Little soul-searching will be required for that claim to be realized; rather, it will be a matter of determining ways of attaining professional confidence. Despite having experienced a distinct lack of appreciation from the public over the years (including the press, on occasion), teachers will need to gather momentum towards declaring themselves as competent operators of the pedagogical process. Once this is accomplished, an appeal for proper recognition can be made to government to implement the autonomous plan.

Any suggestion to amend the present system of educational hierarchy as we know it will, of course, be met with a measure of objection from various quarters. There will be complaints that the plan will encourage a degree of variation beyond that which the system can withstand. This criticism can be countered with reference to the fact that certain standards of education will be maintained throughout the system. Furthermore, variation is a fact in a pluralistic society and as such should be reflected in the schools. There will also be complaints that the representation of the public via trusteeship must be maintained to ensure the democratic rights of society. Again, these critics will need to be reminded that no profession other than teaching (and there are several which deal with children) have that kind of a "safeguard" operating against them. Also, the plan calls for a strengthened role for parents directly, not a diminished one. Finally, the state, as always, through its elected representatives, constitutes a measure of assurance against possible abuse in the same way that it functions in relation to other professions.

Criticisms aside, the bottom line of educational reform is what happens to the children for whom these institutions are designed. Presumably, this is what it is all about, and if there is anything that can be done that will enhance their learning opportunities, it should be undertaken. One area that has not yet been explored in this regard is what will happen when the floodgates of pedagogy are opened to release the previously constricted powers of the teaching profession. That avenue has the guarantee that since no other single segment of society has a greater passion for the best interests of the child at heart, the more quickly it is accomplished, the better. Reforming the schools "for teachers" will ultimately provide the best advantages for today's child.

A Reform Grid

The following procedures outline the progression of necessary moves toward professional autonomy and clearly reveal the logic and ease by which the plan may be implemented.

1. Develop and promote a sense of urgency among members of the teaching profession to claim the right and the

opportunity to develop professionally by attaining a greater degree of autonomy in the operation of schools.

2. Obtain a commitment from the Ministry or Department of Education to honor the petition of the teaching profession for greater autonomy by consenting to and negotiating the implemention of the plan for autonomous education on a pilot basis in an appropriate community.

3. Identify a local steering committee of teachers to design a format for implementation of the plan in terms of school(s) location, administrative design, philosophy of education, level of education - elementary, junior high or senior high school, etc.

4. Have the plan approved by the government department in conjunction with consultation with local community parent representatives or groups.

5. Communicate the message of the new school(s) to the local constituency so that the element of choice in education is clearly understood.

6. Maintain the present financial arrangement for funding schooling until an evaluation and analysis of the pilot project can be completed and any shortcoming rectified. Pilot schools could be regarded as alternative settings within a regular system for an interim period of time.

7. Establish a formula or method by which evaluations may be utilized as a means of bringing about a complete system of professionally controlled education which will enhance pupil learning, furnish real choice and increase parental input. This combination will constitute genuine reform in education; it will be a first and it is a must!

## FOOTNOTES

[1] David K. Cohen, "Tendencies in Public School Governance", in Future Trends in Education Policy, Jane Newitt, Ed. Lexington, Mass.: Lexington Books, 1979, 125-142.

[2] R.S. Downie, et.al., Education and Personal Relationships: A Philosophical Study. London: Methuen, 1974, 101.

[3] Bruce R. Joyce, Alternative Models of Elementary Education. Waltham, Mass.: Blaisdell, 1969, 29-31.

[4] Ralph M. Kimbrough suggests that the myth of group dynamics in the early 1940s led many educators to believe that simply involving people in the educational process was somehow beneficial. See his Political Power and Educational Decision-Making. Chicago: Rand McNally, 1964, 2-3.

[5] The Quebec School:  A Responsible Force in the Community, Ministere de l'Education, Gouvernement du Quebec, 1982, 52.

[6] Martin Mayer, The Schools. New York:  Anchor Books, 1961, 23.

[7] Don Adams, Schooling and Social Change in Modern America. New York:  Don McKay, 1972, 221.

[8] Leo Anglin et.al., Teaching:  What It's About, New York:  Harper and Row, 1982, 252.

ABOUT THE AUTHOR

John W. Friesen is a Professor in the Department of Educational Policy and Administrative Studies at The University of Calgary where he has taught since 1967. He is the author of numerous books and articles on multiculturalism and education, including *When Cultures Clash* (1985), *The Cultural Maze* (1987), *The Dicare of Canada* (1988), *The Cultural Dilemma* (1989) *Readings in Canadian History* (1991), *When Cultures Clash* (revised edition, 1993).

He is a member of the American Sociological Association and the Alberta Historical Guild and editor of the Multicultural Education Journal.